CUTTING AND

D0884631

CUTTING AND SETTING STONES

by HERBERT SCARFE

WATSON-GUPTILL PUBLICATIONS – NEW YORK

First published in the United States of America 1972
by *Watson Guptill Publications*, a division of
Billboard Publications Inc, *165 West 46 Street, New York, NY*

Copyright © 1972 by Herbert Scarfe

First published 1972 in Great Britain
by *B T Batsford Limited*
4 Fitzhardinge Street, London W1H 0AH

Manufactured in Great Britain
First printing 1972

Library of Congress Cataloging in Publication Data

Scarfe, Herbert
Cutting and Setting Stones
Bibliography:
1 Gem cutting.   2 Jewelry making.   I Title
TS752.5.S27   736',2   72–3356
ISBN 0–8230–1150–X

CONTENTS

Acknowledgment   7

Introduction   8

Suitable gemstone material   9
   Cabochons and flat sections   10
   Tumbling   10
   Facetting   11

Preparation of gemstone rough   17

Cutting and setting cabochons   24
   Cutting procedure   28
   Setting cabochons   37

Polishing flat sections   45
   Drilling stones   49
   Setting flat sections   50

Faceted stones and their settings   54
   Facetting equipment   54
   Cutting laps   57
   Polishing laps   57
   Polishes   58
   Cutting a standard brilliant   58
   Cutting sequences   59
   Shaping the girdle   62
   The table   62
   Crown main facets   64
   Table star facets   65
   Crown girdle facets   66
   Polishing the crown facets   66
   Use of transfer block   66
   Method of transfer   66
   Pavilion main facets   70
   Girdle facets   70
   Polishing the pavilion facets   70
   Removing stone from dopstick   70
   Care of facetting equipment   70

Mounting faceted stones   71
Box settings   72
Coronet settings   72
Pavé or bead settings   72

Tumbled stones and baroque jewelry   74
Working procedure for rotary tumblers   76
Vibratory tumblers   78
Working procedure for vibratory tumblers   79
Mounting tumble-polished stones   79
Findings   80
Assembling a pendant   80
Making a chain bracelet   82
Flat pad bracelet   82

Natural crystals in jewelry   84

Design   85
Use of stones in creative jewelry   85

Jewelry tools and materials   92
Metals and solders   92
Heating   92
Some basic equipment   92
Acid bath or 'pickle'   93
Polishing   93

Further reading   94

Suppliers   95

ACKNOWLEDGMENT

Thanks are due to my wife, Doreen, for her assistance during the preparation of the manuscript; to friends and colleagues for their encouragement and also to Mr Eric Johnson of Hull for his patience in taking the photographs for figures 3, 4, 14, 16, 18–20, 22–25, 33, 34, 66 and 68.

Acknowledgment is made to the following firms by whose courtesy their photographs are reproduced:
Gemrocks Limited, London, figure 41
Geode Industries Inc, New London, Iowa, figures 8, 36, 64 and 65
Highland Park Manufacturing Division, Musto Industries Inc, Hawthorne, California, figures 7 and 62
A. D. Hughes Limited, Warley, Worcestershire, figure 42
Kernowcraft Rocks and Gems Limited, Truro, Cornwall, figures 5, 12 and 61
PMR Lapidary Equipment and Supplies, Pitlochry, Perthshire, figures 6, 9 and 10
Star Diamond Industries Inc, California, figure 60
Wessex Impex Limited, UK agent, Winchester, figures 11 and 35.

The help and courtesy of manufacturers and suppliers of lapidary equipment, is greatly appreciated. Machines used in the cutting and polishing sequences were kindly loaned by Gemstones of Hull and PMR Lapidary Equipment and Supplies, Pitlochry.

HS
Long Riston 1972

INTRODUCTION

Lapidary is now firmly established as a leisure pursuit for people of all ages and as an educational craft in schools. Many amateur lapidaries are extending their interests to jewelry-making; closely relating the combined skills and disciplines demanded in both cutting and setting stones. The principal aims of this book are to meet these demands and associate cutting and polishing specific stone shapes with appropriate methods of mounting in jewelry. Consideration of design factors and the many sources of visual stimulus available for creative jewelry will encourage further exploration and inventiveness.

Although not a book on jewelry techniques, progressive stages in developing traditional settings are introduced to support the basic theme of mounting or securing gemstones in such a way that the qualities of the stones are displayed to advantage.

SUITABLE GEMSTONE MATERIAL

Precious stones used in jewelry, notably diamond, sapphire, ruby and emerald, are cut from minerals of crystalline structure which owe their value as gem material to extreme hardness, rarity and certain optical properties which are revealed and enhanced through correct cutting. Many other stones, including topaz, tourmaline, amethyst and citrine, display equally attractive features when cut and polished. In this secondary group, rough material of suitable quality for cutting may be far more accessible to the amateur gem-cutter.

Stones for experimental as well as orthodox jewelry styles can be chosen on their decorative merits and ornamental stones from world-wide sources are frequently selected for colour and texture as a basis for creative design. Many beach pebbles, although of no intrinsic value, have subtlety of shape and pattern which gives them unique attraction when polished.

The hardness of gem materials, or their resistance to abrasion, is an important factor in the selection of stones for lapidary purposes. These must be suitable for cutting by one of the recognised processes, which in every case involves shaping and refining by progressive stages of abrasion. The order of hardness for some minerals, based on Mohs' scale, is given for comparisons, although in no way representing the degrees of hardness between one mineral and another.

TABLE 1 MOHS' SCALE		COMPARATIVE HARDNESS OF SOME OTHER MINERALS	
1	Talc		
2	Gypsum	$2\frac{1}{2}$	Amber
3	Calcite	$3\frac{1}{2}$	Jet
4	Fluorite	4	Malachite, rhodochrosite
5	Apatite	5	Obsidian
		$5\frac{1}{2}$	Lapis lazuli, opal
6	Orthoclase	$6\frac{1}{2}$	Peridot
7	Quartz	$7\frac{1}{2}$	Tourmaline, emerald
8	Topaz	$8\frac{1}{2}$	Alexandrite
9	Corundum { Ruby / Sapphire	$9\frac{1}{4}$	Silicon carbide (*man-made abrasive*)
10	Diamond	$9\frac{1}{2}$	Boron carbide (*man-made abrasive*)

As a general rule, stones used for cutting domed cabochons and flat sections are opaque or transluscent and usually below hardness 8 on Mohs' scale. Polished cabochons reflect light from the surface, showing characteristic lustre such as glassy, waxy, metallic, etc. Opaque stones may be cut to display variety of colour and intricacy of surface pattern, such as flow-banding of coloured oxides seen in jasper and the many forms of agate. Transluscent stones reveal a depth of reflected colour or fascinating play of light on the internal structure of the mineral, producing qualities of asterism or chatoyance. The moving bands of light observed in polished tiger's-eye are the result of light falling on the silky fibres of silica-replaced asbestos in the composition of the stone. Most beautiful of all stones are precious opals, reflecting iridescence from the microlayered structure.

An extensive range of gemstone rough from many parts of the world is imported by an increasing number of lapidary suppliers. If access to a diamond saw is possible, it is cheaper to buy rock in bulk. Rock bought in lumps will have been hammered from larger pieces, which may have resulted in flaws and fractures within the stone, and careful inspection of the rough is recommended before purchase. Material which has already been sawn into thin slabs by the dealer is sold by the square inch. When selecting slabs for cabochons it is important to make sure the slice is of sufficient thickness to allow for the dome. If the slab is to be polished as a flat section thickness is not so important, although very thin slices are more liable to fracture during cutting. Beaches, stream-beds, quarries and gravel pits are also prolific sources of interesting stones suitable for polishing, and small pebbles can be sliced on a trim-saw prior to shaping.

TUMBLING

Most stones suitable for cabochons are also used for tumbling and obtained from the same sources. Off-cuts from sawing and pieces of rock too small or uneven for cabochons can be polished together in rotary tumblers providing they are of similar hardness. The most satisfactory results are produced by using good quality material which is free from cracks, holes and other imperfections. Smooth water-worn pebbles selected for tumbling should be of hard, compact structure and non-absorbent.

FACETTING

High quality gem material is expensive and may be difficult to obtain by the amateur gem-cutter. Flawless crystals of large size are unusual, which accounts for the small dimensions of many cut stones. Crystalline quartz varieties such as rock crystal, smoky quartz, citrine and amethyst can be bought from most lapidary suppliers and will provide an excellent basis for practice and acquisition of facetting skills. A further reason for the suitability of quartz as an introductory mineral for facetting is the absence of cleavage planes. Many stones have to be meticulously orientated to position the facets correctly in relation to the planes of cleavage but this does not apply to the quartz varieties.

FIGURE I   Refraction and internal reflection of light in a standard brilliant cut

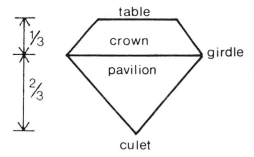

A   Standard brilliant

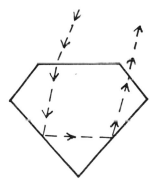

B   Path of light ray entering and leaving the crown, reflecting internally from the back facets

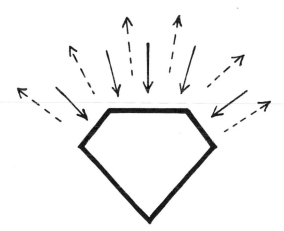

C   Light enters and leaves the crown in all directions, giving a reflected brilliance as the stone is moved

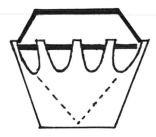

D   A brilliant, mounted in a coronet setting, allowing the crown maximum exposure to light

Facetting rough is usually sold by the ounce or carat and avoidance of waste is an important consideration. Although it may be possible to select crystals which are of good shape and relatively smooth, very often the material has broken with uneven fractures and has sharp points and ridges which have to be removed during pre-forming.

Transparent gem minerals used for facetting possess certain refractive properties within the structure which allows light to enter the cut stones from above and be reflected from the back facets, returning maximum sparkle or 'fire' in correctly faceted stones (figure 1). This important optical property can be measured and tables showing the refractive index for different minerals are given in books dealing with gemmology and mineralogy.

Good grade facetting rough can be selected by carrying out simple tests. Transparent crystals with polished natural faces present few problems and by orientation in a good light it is a simple matter to detect any inclusions or internal fractures which may be present. Examination of material with unevenly fractured surfaces can be carried out by holding it against a strong light to illuminate the interior of the stone, and shading the eyes from direct light glare. By slowly rotating the rough in the light beam, imperfections can usually be observed. A further method for inspection of transparent medium is by immersion in clear fluid which has a similar refractive index to the gem rough. The fractured edges of the material will not be visible when fully immersed and a strong light passing through the container (a clear glass jar) will reveal the presence of any flaws which interrupt the passage of light and spread the light rays. Coloured crystalline material must be examined with care to ensure even distribution of colour throughout the crystal. Patchy colouration should not be confused with colour zoning which is a feature in some gemstones, for example tourmaline can display bands of pink, green and blue in the same crystal.

Synthetic gem material suitable for facetting displays many of the recognised characteristics of natural gemstones. The differences between natural and synthetic gems can be determined by carrying out scientific tests for colour and internal structural variations. Cutting is carried out in the same manner as for natural crystals, although in some cases a higher refractive index might have to be allowed for when calculating facet angles.

The following short list showing characteristics of popular stones suitable for cutting cabochons, tumbling and facetting is intended only as a guide and additional varieties are available from suppliers of rocks and minerals.

TABLE 2   A SHORT LIST OF POPULAR STONES

AGATE VARIETIES *Cryptocrystalline quartz*	H7 Heat sensitivity medium to high.
Banded, fortification, orbicular	White to pale blue chalcedony with red, brown, black, yellow or green banding, and circular patterns.
Moss agate	Clear transluscent chalcedony with green, red or blue moss-like inclusions.
Dendritic or tree agate	White to pale brown, opaque. Compact material with dendritic inclusions of bright green, brown or black, resembling branches or tree growth.
Plume and flame agate	Transluscent. Fused colouration suggesting feathers or smoke and flames.
Scenic agate	Opaque – transluscent. Inclusions suggest landscape features.
Lace agate	Opaque – transluscent. Finely banded in intricate lacy patterns.
AMAZONITE *Microcline feldspar*	H6 Pale to dark turquoise green. Has characteristic schiller effect when correctly orientated.
AVENTURINE *Crystalline quartz*	H7 Light to deep green, blue. Transluscent. Contains silvery flecks of mica.
BLOODSTONE *Cryptocrystalline quartz*	H7 Opaque. Dark green spotted with red. Brittle and liable to flake.

TABLE 2 *continued*

CHALCEDONY *Cryptocrystalline quartz*	H6½–7 Milky white to pale blue. Transluscent. Compact, heat sensitive.
Carnelian	Transluscent. Orange to deep red.
Chrysoprase	Transluscent. Bright green.
Jasper	Opaque. Chalcedony fused with coloured impurities. Red, green, yellow to brown. Sometimes contains streaks of haematite. Subject to undercutting due to soft and hard areas in the mixed mineral composition.
LAPIS LAZULI *Lazurite*	H5 Opaque. Ultramarine blue flecked with iron pyrites. Inferior quality is streaked with grey and white calcite.
MALACHITE *Copper carbonate*	H3–4 Opaque. Deep to pale green. Ribbon and orbicular banding. Care needed in cutting – liable to separate on banding line due to layered formation.
MOSS OR DENDRITIC OPAL *Opalised silica*	H6–7 Opaque. Vitreous lustre. Pale to deep yellow ochre, blue-grey, with moss-like dendrites of deeper colour. Brittle and heat sensitive.
OBSIDIAN *Volcanic glass*	H5 Amorphous. Opaque to transluscent. Intense black to mahogany brown. Colour can be evenly distributed or striped, smoky with rainbow sheen. Star-like inclusions of white or grey known as Snowflake obsidian. Smoky brown nodules known as 'Apache tears'. Brittle, chips easily.
OPAL *Hydrated silica*	H5½–6½ Amorphous. Precious opal shows play of spectrum colours, varying in intensity. Heat sensitive and brittle.

TABLE 2 *continued*

PETRIFIED WOOD (*many varieties*)	Mineral replacement of wood by agate, jasper or opal. Hardness varies according to composition.
RHODOCHROSITE *Manganese carbonate*	H4 Opaque. Banded and orbicular patterns. Pink to deep red with white. Satin sheen.
RHODONITE *Manganese silicate*	H5–6 Opaque. Pale pink to red, veined with black or yellow. Tough and compact.
ROSE QUARTZ *Crystalline quartz*	H7 Transluscent. Pale pink. Heat sensitive. Often has internal fractures.
RUTILATED QUARTZ *Crystalline quartz*	H7 Transparent, with inclusions of golden rutile needles.
SODALITE *Sodium aluminium silicate*	$H5\frac{1}{2}$–6 Opaque. Light to deep blue streaked with white or grey. Brittle.
TIGER'S-EYE *Silicified asbestos*	H7 Opaque. Golden yellow to brown, blue to green, red. Silky fibres give chatoyance.
TOURMALINE IN QUARTZ *Crystalline quartz*	H7 Transparent, with needle-like inclusions of black tourmaline.

NOTE FOR READERS IN AUSTRALIA AND THE USA
Natural deposits of most of the ornamental and gem minerals mentioned in TABLE 2 and TABLE 3 occur in various parts of Australia and the USA and suitable specimens for cutting may be collected in the field by the amateur.

TABLE 3   GEM MINERALS TO FACET   H–Hardness (Mohs' scale)   RI–Refractive Index

APATITE H5 RI 1.64	Green, yellow, blue, colourless. Heat sensitive, brittle.
BERYL VARIETIES H7$\frac{1}{2}$–8 RI 1.57–1.59	Emerald, deep green. Aquamarine, blue to green. Not heat sensitive.
GARNET H6$\frac{1}{2}$–7$\frac{1}{2}$ RI 1.7–1.9	Several varieties. Yellow, orange, green, deep red, purple red.
PERIDOT H6$\frac{1}{2}$–7 RI 1.67	Yellow-green. Not heat sensitive.
QUARTZ VARIETIES H7 RI 1.55 *Amethyst* – Purple *Smoky* – Brown, grey-black *Citrine* – Yellow *Rock crystal* – Colourless	Heat sensitive. No cleavage planes.
SPINEL H8 RI 1.72	Yellow, red, blue, purple. Low heat sensitivity.
TOPAZ H8 RI 1.61–1.63	Colourless, blue, yellow to brown, pink. Not heat sensitive.
TOURMALINE H7–7$\frac{1}{2}$ RI 1.62–1.64	Colourless, light and dark green, blue, pink, red, brown, black. Heat sensitive.
ZIRCON H7–7$\frac{1}{2}$ RI 1.78–1.98	Colourless, blue, green, yellow, brown, red. Brittle.
STRONTIUM TITANATE H6$\frac{1}{2}$ RI 2.41	A colourless man-made stone with no natural counterpart.
SYNTHETIC CORUNDUM H9 RI 1.76	Synthetic ruby and sapphire. Also in colours simulating danburite, rose topaz, tourmaline, etc.
SYNTHETIC SPINEL H8 RI 1.72	In colours simulating aquamarine, peridot, tourmaline, zircon and red spinel.
SYNTHETIC RUTILE H6$\frac{1}{2}$–7 RI 2.62	Colourless, high dispersion.
YTTRIUM ALUMINIUM GARNET H7$\frac{1}{2}$ RI 1.83	A man-made stone with no natural counterpart.

PREPARATION OF GEMSTONE ROUGH

Large rocks have to be reduced to workable sizes and in the first instance this is usually accomplished by hammering. It is important to keep the amount of hammering to a minimum in order to avoid the risk of fractures occurring within the material. When the pieces are of reasonable size they should be further reduced by means of a slabbing saw to produce manageable rock slices. These slabs are then trimmed to convenient shapes on a trim-saw (figures 2 and 3). Crystalline material intended for facetting should be cut with a fine gauge trim-saw blade.

Saw blades are thin metal discs with particles of diamond embedded in the rim. There are two types of blade in general use: the notched rim, with diamond in sealed notches, and the sintered rim, with diamond particles and powdered metal fused to the periphery of the blade. In both cases the rim is thicker than the rest of the disc in order to allow a clearance when cutting, otherwise the blade may become wedged in the saw-cut.

The effective cutting action of a blade can be maintained by periodically clearing the burrs of metal which may have been dragged over the diamond points as a result of repeated sawing through hard stones such as agate. A few slices cut through a soft sand-brick, mortar, or a worn soft-bonded grinding wheel is usually sufficient to expose the diamond. Some manufacturers recommend occasional reversal of the blade to ensure even wear on the cutting edge.

Saw blades can either be mounted in a vertical position on a horizontal shaft and revolve through an oily coolant contained in a small tank, or can operate horizontally with an overhead drip-feed of water or light oil. A fifty-fifty mixture of light flushing oil and paraffin is a suitable coolant. When sawing with an oily mixture, the stones should be washed in warm water and detergent immediately after cutting to prevent oil being absorbed. For stones of a highly absorbent nature, such as turquoise and opal, water should always be used as the coolant.

FIGURE 2 Diagrammatic sequence of
preparing rough

B Sharp points may have to be removed
on grinding wheel, to provide flat base
for sawing

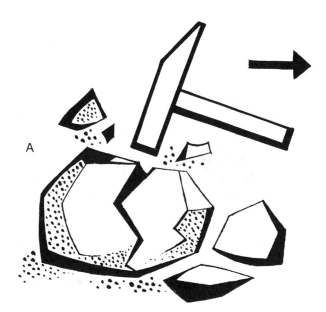

A Rock hammered into workable pieces

C Stone can now be slabbed into required
slices, using a diamond saw

D Agate nodules are best sawn in preference to hammering, in order to prevent internal shattering

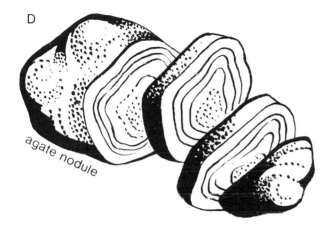

D

agate nodule

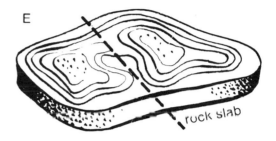

E

rock slab

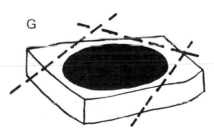

G

dotted lines show direction of saw cuts

E, F AND G Slabs should be trimmed to isolate the best features and use the stone economically. Corners can be trimmed away to save excessive grinding

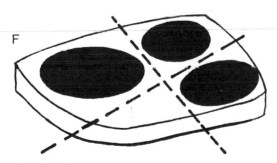

F

3 cabochons marked out

FIGURE 3   A rock slice marked for cutting on a trim saw. The agate pattern shows a convenient position for two stones

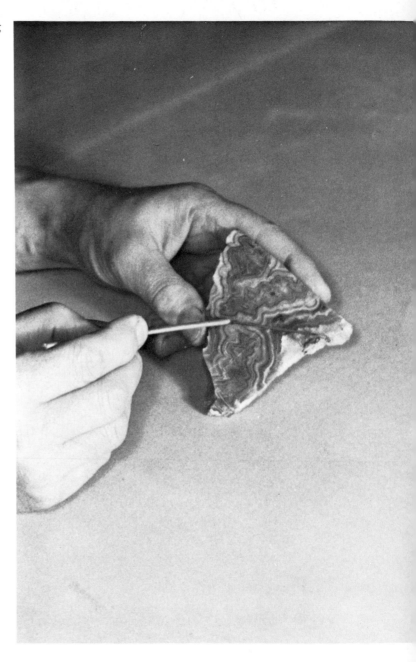

During trimming, slabs and small pebbles can be safely held in the fingers and fed gently to the revolving blade by pushing the stone along the flat saw bed (figure 4). Splash guards in front of the saw bed and over the blade are essential to protect the operator from spray during cutting on the vertical saw. These are usually adequately provided on manufactured diamond saws, and on some larger saws plastic canopies completely enclose the saw bed, eliminating any coolant spray.

FIGURE 5 (opposite top left)   Use of a rock clamp for cutting on a horizontal saw. Note overhead drip-feed tap for coolant. Australian *Robilt Gem-maker*

FIGURE 6 (opposite top right)   Slabbing and trimming saw with 203 mm (8 in.) blade, showing a rock clamp and guide rail. *Manufactured by PMR Lapidary Equipment and Supplies, Pitlochry, Perthshire*

Do not attempt to hold the stone in the fingers when trimming on a horizontal blade as the degree of control is limited, and use of a rock-clamp is essential (figure 5). Another type of saw has a gravity feed which, in addition to being effortless, enables cutting to proceed at the same regulated speed and produces sliced faces which are free from saw marks. Tension on the gravity feed slowly moves the rock vise carriage forward, holding the rock against the blade (figure 7).

Very high speeds are not required for sawing as excessive frictional heat can damage both blade and stone. Harder materials should be cut at reduced speeds and softer varieties may be cut at slightly higher speeds. A reduced speed will also lessen the amount of coolant spray from the blade, which is a further advantage. The diamond blade, which should be immersed in the coolant to a depth of approximately 6 mm to 10 mm ($\frac{1}{4}$ in. to $\frac{3}{8}$ in.), must never be allowed to cut dry, and at faster speeds the coolant level in the tank may require frequent renewal. At the end of the sawing operation, surplus fluid should be drained away and accumulated sludge and rock fragments removed from the tank.

FIGURE 7 (opposite bottom left)   Slabbing and trimming saw with a gravity feed controlled rock clamp. The clamp is pulled slowly along the guide rail (to right of saw bed) by means of a weighted tension wire (not shown). *Highland Park Model E-2*

FIGURE 8 (opposite bottom right)   An unusual saw design which operates at an angle of 45 degrees. Rock clamp is essential. Water coolant in overhead trough is piped to saw blade. *Lortone CCU-6 Gem-making Unit*

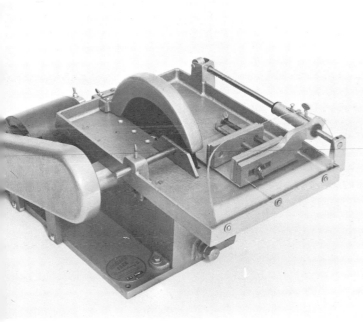

Most manufactured lapidary machines available to the amateur, operate on the same basic principles and with similarities in construction. The illustrated catalogues supplied by dealers display a wide range of equipment for cutting and polishing cabochons (figures 9, 10 and 11). Combined lapidary units incorporate one or two grinding wheels mounted vertically on a horizontal shaft and may also include a diamond saw. On the extended shaft a screw thread accommodates interchangeable discs for sanding and polishing. Grinding wheels must be supplied with water coolant when in use, either by controlled overhead drip-feed or from a trough of water below the wheel.

FIGURE 9   *PMR Twin Grinder*. Water coolant piped to inlet taps over each wheel. This machine shows a chuck extending from the shaft which can accommodate abrasive bits for carving or polishing mops for jewelry making

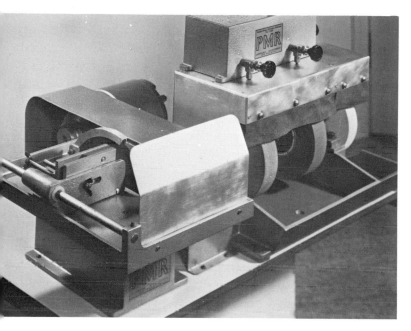

FIGURE 10 *PMR Combination Unit*, incorporating diamond saw, double grinding wheels and sanding and polishing attachments. Note overhead coolant tank with controlled drip-feed to grinding wheels. Drainage hole for surplus liquid can be seen below the wheels

#2095 GP-8
8" GRINDER-POLISHER

FIGURE 11 *Star Diamond GP-8*. Extended cabochon unit. From left to right: Drum sander, two 203 mm (8 in.) diameter grinding wheels, sanding and polishing disc. Coolant piped in from rear, with needle-valve adjustment above wheels. Adjustable hand rests and splash guards. *Manufactured by Star Diamond Industries Inc. USA*

FIGURE 12 Horizontal unit for sawing, grinding, sanding and polishing. Adjustable rock clamp and coolant container. Triple pulley system for machine speed changes can be seen. Australian *Robilt Gem-maker*

An alternative type of machine has horizontal grinding, sanding and polishing wheels on a vertical shaft. Coolant is directed on the wheel from a container fixed in a convenient position (figure 12). For both types of machines, the power is supplied by a small electric motor, $\frac{1}{6}$ hp or $\frac{1}{4}$ hp. A belt and triple pulley system will provide suitable changes of speed (figures 13 and 14). As a general guide, the grinding operations are carried out at double the motor speed, sanding at motor speed, and the polishing phase at half the motor speed.

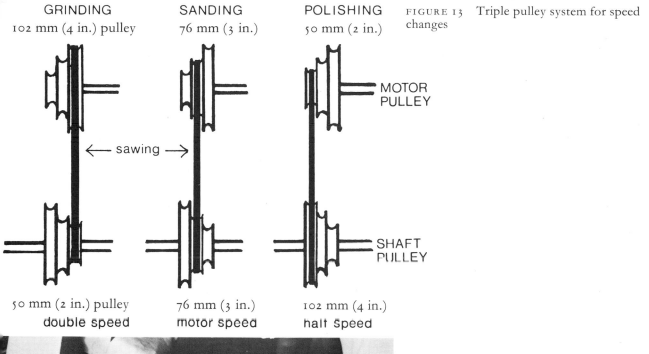

GRINDING	SANDING	POLISHING	
102 mm (4 in.) pulley	76 mm (3 in.)	50 mm (2 in.)	

FIGURE 13   Triple pulley system for speed changes

MOTOR PULLEY

← sawing →

SHAFT PULLEY

50 mm (2 in.) pulley	76 mm (3 in.)	102 mm (4 in.)
double speed	**motor speed**	**half speed**

FIGURE 14   Changing the operational speeds for different processes is a simple matter, with a multiple pulley system on motor and shaft. Holding the belt in both hands as shown, ease it across to corresponding pulleys as required

27

The grinding wheels, abrasive grits and coated abrasive wet/dry papers used in conjunction with the machines, are composed of silicon carbide. This is man-made, with a hardness of $9\frac{1}{4}$ (see Table 1), and is capable of grinding all stones of hardness 8 and below. Grit particles in the composition of the wheels have a vitreous bonding produced at high temperatures, making the wheels extremely tough but allowing variations of soft, medium and hard bond. The soft and medium bonded wheels should be used for cutting hard stones, allowing the worn grit particles to fall away and expose new cutting edges, thus speeding up the cutting action. Hard bonded grinding wheels make little impression on hard stones and the surface of the wheel tends to become glazed. Silicon carbide grinding wheels, loose abrasive and wet/dry papers are manufactured in a wide range of grit sizes from coarse to fine. For the grinding stages it is usually sufficient to obtain 100 and 220 grit wheels. Sanding phases can be carried out on 220 and 400 grit wet/dry papers or 220, 320 and 500 grades if using loose abrasive grits. As the grit size numbers increase, the grits become finer until in the upper grades they are classed as *flours*.

CUTTING PROCEDURE

Cabochons are shaped roughly and refined using different grades of grinding wheels, followed by stages of abrasion on sanding discs, until the surface is perfectly smooth. Successive stages should eliminate any marks left by the previous abrasive stage. Final polishing is accomplished with a polishing agent such as cerium oxide, zirconium oxide or tin oxide, mixed with water to a thin paste and applied to a leather or felt disc.

Grinding wheels should never be used without an adequate supply of water coolant to prevent stones overheating and cracking, also to avoid softening of dopping wax and displacement of the stone from the dopstick. Wheels must never be left in the water when not in use, as moisture absorbed weakens the bonding and makes the wheel susceptible to crumbling or flaking. If a wheel has been left standing in water, it should be allowed to revolve at grinding speed for a short period to dry off excess moisture prior to use.

When cutting on vertical wheels, avoid severe grooving of the front cutting edge by utilising the whole of the grinding surface. Grinding into the side of the wheel must not occur under any circumstances, as any deep grooving near the edge creates a dangerously sharp corner which is liable to break away. Grooves in the front cutting edge of the wheel can be removed by using a wheel dressing tool.

At sanding stages, wet/dry discs are fixed to a rubber backing pad on metal sanding laps with a peel-off gum solution. Water coolant is necessary during sanding for most stones, although some materials, such as haematite, jet and jade, will achieve a high polish on a dry, well-worn sanding disc. Frequent inspections of the stone should be made as sanding progresses.

Another, and more economical, method of sanding is the use of loose abrasive grit powders on horizontal discs. The discs can be made of thin leather glued to a resilient rubber or felt pad, with a plywood or perspex base for support. A separate disc is required for each grade of grit used and these should be stored in individual polythene bags. Silicon carbide grit powder is mixed with water and applied to the revolving disc from a squeezy bottle, or with a small brush. Slow speeds are required to prevent the grit being thrown from the discs. The three sanding phases, using 220, 320 and 500 grades of loose grit successively, should be followed by final polishing. It is important to wash hands and stone carefully between grit stages, and before commencing polishing, make sure that all traces of grit are removed from working surfaces to avoid transferring any grit particles to the polishing pad.

When ready for the final polishing stage, mix a thin paste of polishing agent and water and apply this to the felt or leather pad when in motion. Do not over-saturate, as the polishing or glazing period occurs when the pad is almost dry. Excessive moisture will only cause the stone to skid over the surface. Frictional heat, which may crack the stone, can result from too much pressure on a dry felt disc and more polishing paste should be applied as required. It is advisable to lift the stone from the polishing pad frequently to allow the stone to cool. If all the previous stages of grinding and sanding have been carried out thoroughly, the stone will soon acquire a high

FIGURE 15 Sequences for cutting and
polishing a cabochon, using saw and
combination lapidary unit

polish, but it is not possible to polish out imperfections or
scratches. Should any scratches remain present, it will be
necessary to return to the sanding stages to remove them before
a perfect polish can be achieved.

It is possible to hold the stone in the fingers throughout the
various stages, but it makes for ease of manipulation to mount
it on a dopstick after grinding the base shape. Dopsticks can
be made from short lengths of wooden dowel and the stone
is secured with dopping wax. This is a mixture of sealing-wax
and powdered shellac, heated in a shallow tin. Suggested
heating arrangements are shown in figure 17.

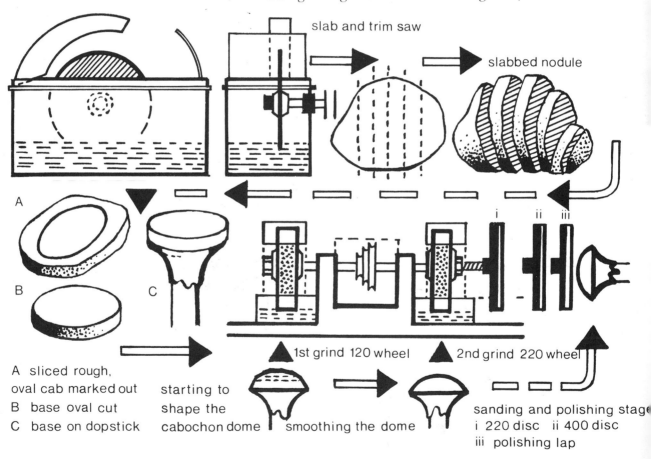

slab and trim saw

slabbed nodule

A

B

C

i   ii   iii

1st grind 120 wheel   2nd grind 220 wheel

A sliced rough,
   oval cab marked out
B base oval cut
C base on dopstick

starting to
shape the
cabochon dome   smoothing the dome

sanding and polishing stage
 i 220 disc   ii 400 disc
 iii polishing lap

FIGURE 16 Using a template, the cabochon base shape is marked out on the slab. The base shape is then ground on the front edge of the grinding wheel as shown. Move the stone across the whole width of the wheel to avoid grooving the cutting surface. Do not grind into the side of the wheel. Finally, a small bevel is cut on the perimeter of the base, prior to dopping. This prevents the edge of the stone chipping during setting

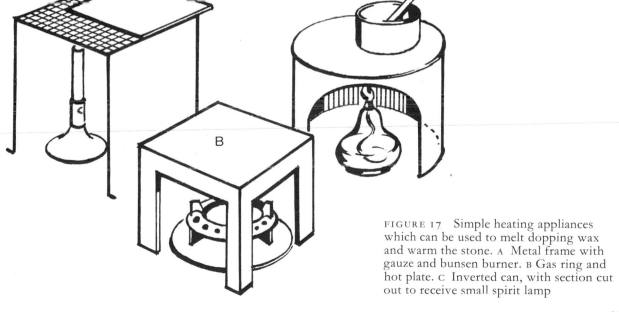

FIGURE 17 Simple heating appliances which can be used to melt dopping wax and warm the stone. A Metal frame with gauze and bunsen burner. B Gas ring and hot plate. C Inverted can, with section cut out to receive small spirit lamp

31

FIGURE 18 Dopsticks of various sizes prepared for use by dipping in hot wax and standing, wax end down, on a cool surface. The wax makes a conical support for the stone. Additional wax may be used as reinforcement. A stick of suitable size has been selected and the wax re-softened in a flame. The stone to be dopped is warming on the hot-plate

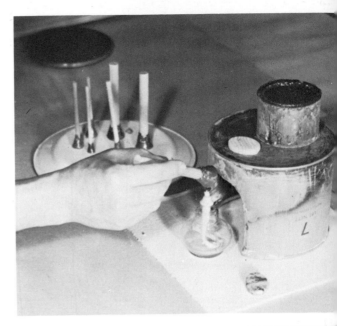

FIGURE 19 (below left) When the wax begins to melt on the dopstick, press wax on the stone and lift clear of the hot-plate. To avoid over-heating, a few grains of powdered shellac sprinkled on the stone, will indicate the right temperature for dopping as the shellac begins to melt

FIGURE 20 (below right) Lift dopstick and stone upright and mould softened wax into a firm support under the stone. Centre the stone, removing any wax which may spread over the edges, as this may be the cause of unpolished areas. Allow wax and stone to cool thoroughly

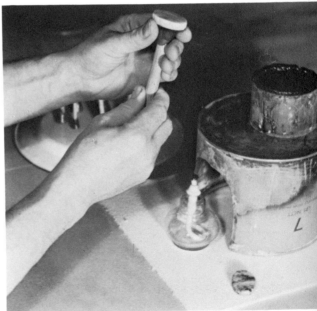

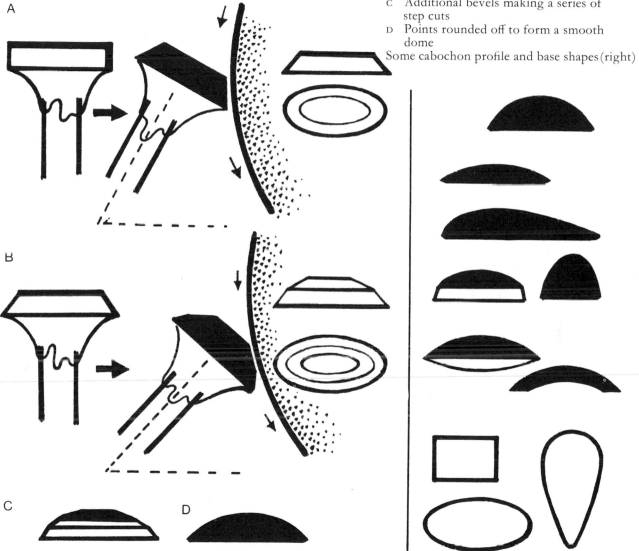

A

B

C   D

FIGURE 21   Stages in shaping the cabochon
dome
A   Angle of first cut, bevelling stone at
    about 45 degrees
B   Change of angle, cutting second bevel
C   Additional bevels making a series of
    step cuts
D   Points rounded off to form a smooth
    dome
Some cabochon profile and base shapes (right)

33

FIGURE 22   Smoothing the cabochon
dome. Note position of the hands holding
dopstick. Thumb and forefinger of left
hand near the wax, giving additional
support to stone. To avoid a series of flat
faces on the dome, the stone must be kept
moving against the wheel, using a rolling
action between fingers and thumb of left
hand and rotating the end of the dopstick
with right hand

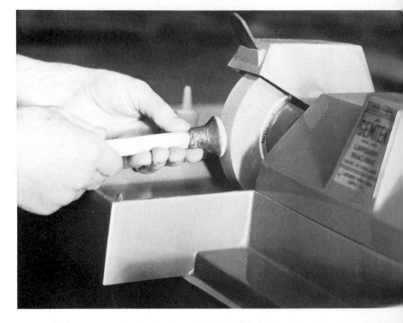

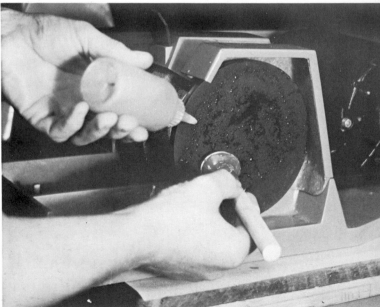

FIGURE 23   Sanding stages using wet/dry
paper discs on a vertical lap. Stone is
rotated against the moving disc using
moderate pressure. Water coolant is
applied from a squeezy bottle as required.
Two stages are usually adequate, using 220
followed by 400 grit disc, prior to final
polishing

34

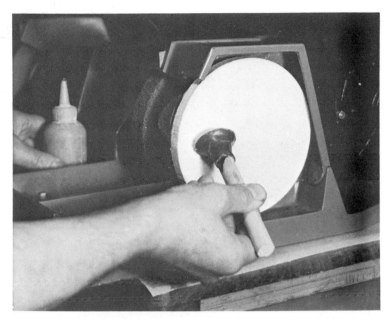

FIGURE 24 Polishing. Tin oxide or cerium oxide mixed with water and applied from squeezy bottle or with soft brush to a disc of leather or thick felt. Never mix oxides together or use on the same disc. Using a circular motion, applying fluctuating pressures against the disc, continue until a polish appears over the entire cabochon surface

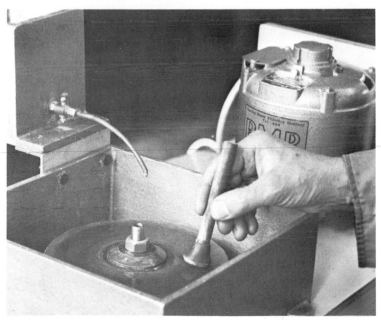

FIGURE 25 Sanding phases on rotating horizontal discs, using wet/dry papers. Grinding wheels and polishing discs are also used horizontally on this type of machine. Water coolant is applied from an overhead container with drip control tap

35

Powdered diamond abrasives and polishing compounds, used by both professional and amateur cutters, can be obtained in several micron sizes for smoothing and polishing cabochons but the finishes obtained with silicon carbide abrasives and various polishing oxides are usually satisfactory for general lapidary purposes. Some cutters combine the two methods; pre-forming the cabochon on a grinding wheel, sanding on wet/dry discs until perfectly smooth, followed by polishing on laps charged with diamond polishing compounds. Although more expensive than usual polishing agents, a small quantity of diamond compound will polish a large number of cabochons and may prove more economical over an extended period.

The composition of laps used with diamond abrasives can vary with the hardness of material being cut and the abrasive stage reached. For domed cabochons, laps of fine-grained wood such as maple, grooved to fit various cabochon sizes, can be used in the early smoothing stages. A coating of wax should be worked into the surface of the wood to retain the diamond particles. Final polishing stages with diamond compounds can be carried out on such materials as leather, felt or padded muslin stretched over a support and the surface well waxed. In order to provide a resilient surface for the curvature of the stone, the lap material should be cushioned on a rubber pad glued to a firm support. Laps used with diamond must be kept solely for that purpose and stored in polythene bags or dust-proof containers. A separate lap must be used for each change in micron size.

In general, the larger micron sizes 45, 30 and 15 are used for smoothing, and the smaller sizes 3 or 1 for polishing, depending on the type of stone being worked. A special extender is used to thin the diamond compound and assist in spreading it over the lap surface. Water lubricant can be applied sparingly to the lap as required. With diamond abrasives the cutting action is speeded up so more frequent inspections are necessary to avoid over-heating or over-cutting the stone.

The following table shows some micron sizes and corresponding grit mesh sizes for diamond compounds. Mesh size is determined by the quantity of grit particles which can be sieved through a screen composed of a fixed number of threads per square inch (square centimetre).

TABLE 4	MICRON SIZE	GRIT MESH SIZE
	1	14,000
	3	8,000
	6	3,000
	15	1,200
	30	600
	45	325

Diamond polishing compounds are supplied in special dispensing syringes with the micron sizes identified by the manufacturers colour code.

CABOCHON SETTINGS

The most satisfactory method of securing a cabochon in a piece of jewelry is by means of the traditional wrap-over or bezel setting. A narrow band of metal shaped round the cabochon base is burnished over the edge of the polished dome, holding the stone tightly in position. The base of the stone rests on a bearer or on a solid metal backing which has been soldered to the bezel. A solid base can be used for opaque stones and the open construction for transluscent stones to allow the passage of light. In this case, elevation of the setting can be used to advantage (see figures 26 and 27 overleaf).

Cabochons with circular, oval or angular base shapes may vary in profile from a shallow convex form to a high dome, and this has a direct influence on the construction of the bezel. A cabochon cut with nearly vertical sides would be unsuitable for a normal wrap-over setting which would allow little or no security for the stone (figure 28). Such stones may either be drilled and pegged at the base or secured in grooves cut in the sides with a fine diamond saw (figure 29). This method can also provide a simple solution for supporting pendant and drop shapes, allowing the stones to be held by wires or metal caps (figure 30). (See pages 40, 41 and 42.)

FIGURE 26 Construction of bezels with open and solid supports for cabochon

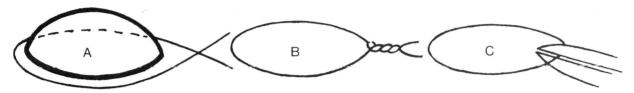

A Circumference of stone measured with binding wire

B Wire pulled tight by twisting
C Wire cut to exact size of cabochon base with tinsnips

D Wire opened out to measure metal strip

E Metal strip moulded around cabochon

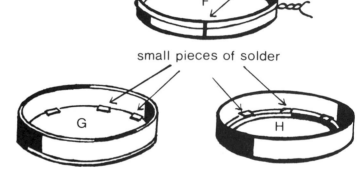

small pieces of solder

F Junction soldered, held in position by binding wire
G Bezel rim now soldered to solid base
H Open bezel, with bearer

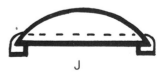

I Rim of bezel filed thin for easy wrap over

J Cabochon set, with bezel firmly wrapped over the stone

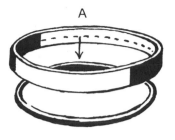

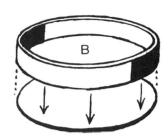

FIGURE 27 Alternative construction of open and solid bezels. The scalloped rim (D) is suitable for very soft or sensitive stones which could not withstand the pressure of a burnisher as used in a continuous wrap over setting

A   Open bezel with bearer
B   Bezel with solid base

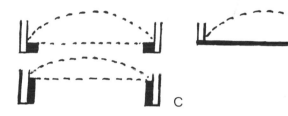

C   Bearer set low and high to allow for shallow or high domed cabochons. Cabochon positions shown in dotted lines

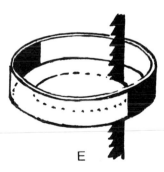

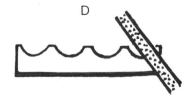

D   Scalloped rim bezel, shaped by filing. The stone is secured by gently pushing over the points

E   Open bezel constructed by piercing a hole in a solid base, to give a wider platform to the stone. Hole cut out with a fine piercing saw

FIGURE 28

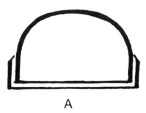

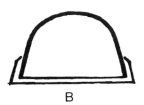

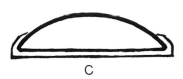

A

B

C

A Cabochons cut with vertical sides cannot be secured by the usual bezel setting

B AND C Stones cut to allow bezel wrap over

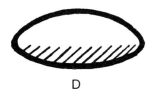

D

D Stones with a double curve, which may be tumbled stones or shaped beach pebbles, can be ground level (shaded area) or cut to receive a special setting

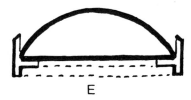

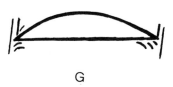

E

F

G

E Small bevel cut around cabochon base facilitates setting

F Stone without a bevel is liable to chip when being set

G Sharp edges dig into sides of metal during setting

A   Angular based stone
B   Irregular shaped cabochons

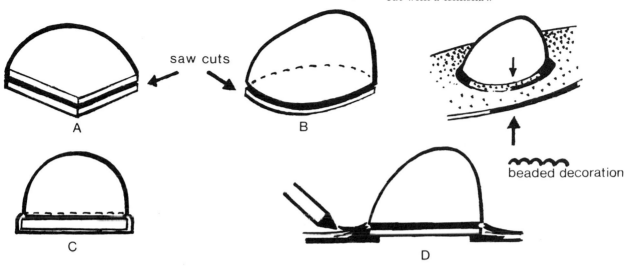

saw cuts

A

B

beaded decoration

C

D

c   Shallow bezel wrapped over and gently tapped into saw cut

D   Metal burred up into saw groove

section of doming block

E

E   Double cabochon secured in a cup setting, formed in a doming block

F

F   Steep cabochons, partly drilled near the base, metal pegs secure the bezel in the drilled hole and gently riveted into position

41

FIGURE 30   Use of small trim-saw and
abrasive-tipped drill for pendant
fastenings
A   Shallow saw groove, secured by
    fine-gauge wire
B   Bell cap can be made to fit a small saw
    cut on the pendant
C   Jump rings and riveted fittings can be
    attached through a drilled hole
D   Small saw cut at the tip of stone, for
    ring or wedge fitting. Clear adhesive
    can be used in conjunction

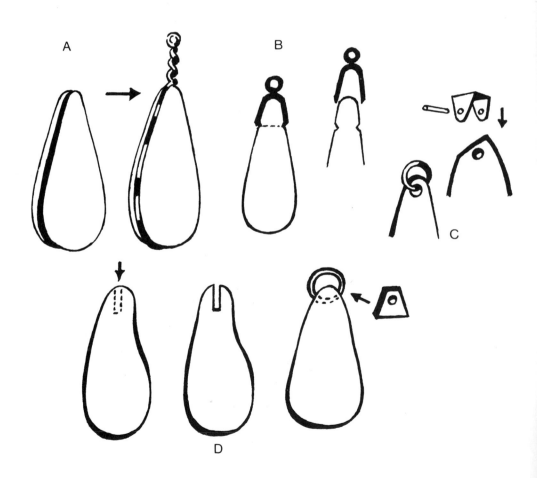

A

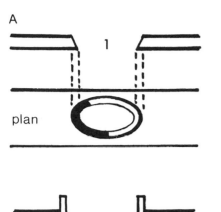

1

plan

2

3

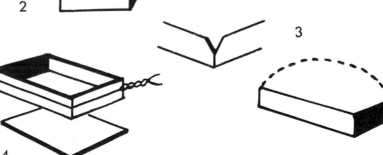

4

FIGURE 31

A Rear setting. Solution to a problem where wrap over bezels on the surface would be difficult, eg when mounting a cluster of high-domed cabochons. Textured surface interest could be added to the metal with a punch or vibratory tool.
1 Tapered hole cut from the rear.
2 Small bezel soldered into a shallow depression. 3 Stone in position, with bezel wrapped over and levelled.
4 Rear set cabochons with textured ground

B Box bezel setting.
1 Cabochon with angular base. 2 Metal strip, bent to shape. 3 Corners with v cut, to meet when wrapped over stone. 4 Box bezel wired up for soldering and base of box setting

B

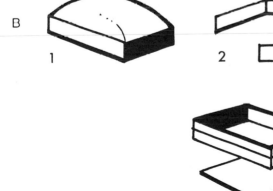

1

2

3

4

When setting clusters of small stones on a shared level support, lack of space between the stones may impede the movements of a burnisher for wrap-over settings. In this case a method frequently used for small faceted stones known as pavé setting can be employed. This involves cutting a shallow seating in the metal to the exact size of the stone, which is inserted into the depression and small burrs of metal are pushed up against it with a graver. The metal burrs are levelled off by gently tapping a punch round the perimeter of the stone. A more decorative effect can be obtained by using a millegrain punch or wheel which forms a pattern of small raised beads in the metal, securing the cabochon in position. Stones can also be set from the rear, as illustrated in figure 31 (see page 43).

In addition to the methods outlined, claws and wire prongs are used as a means of holding a cabochon in position, and stones cut in irregular shapes may suggest more enterprising ways of mounting in creative settings. It should be borne in mind that with lapidary techniques and equipment at his disposal the amateur jeweller can cut stones to suit existing settings, or make modifications to the stones to overcome a problem in setting. This effectively bridges the gap between lapidary and jeweller and provides a finer appreciation of their mutual problems.

POLISHING FLAT SECTIONS

In order to obtain a satisfactory polish on rock slabs and smaller trimmed sections, the surface of the stone must be perfectly smooth to allow the entire surface to be in contact with the lap. Saw marks, hollows and other imperfections should be removed on a non-resilient horizontal lap, using progressively finer abrasives. Cast iron laps are particularly suitable for this purpose, and silicon carbide grits can be applied to the revolving lap with a small brush or squeezy bottle (figure 33). Speeds of 700 rpm or less are recommended to prevent loose abrasive being thrown from the lap. Copper discs impregnated with diamond grits in various grades are also used as an alternative method of abrasion, with water and detergent solution as a coolant.

The flat surface of the stone must be held perfectly level and moved slowly across the lap as cutting proceeds. Even pressure should be applied to the whole slab to avoid rocking or tilting one edge, resulting in a series of small facets on either the leading or trailing edge of the stone. As the speed of the lap near the rim will be faster than the central area, cutting will proceed at variable rates. This must be borne in mind when sanding a large slab and the position of the stone constantly changed to ensure even cutting. Renewal of the grit paste will be necessary as the grit particles are gradually broken down by pressure of the stone. If the slab is too thin to hold comfortably in the fingers it can be gummed to a wooden block of similar proportions until polishing is completed.

The different grades of silicon carbide grit used and the number of changes required to obtain a smooth finish will depend on the condition and hardness of the stone. Combinations such as 80 grit, followed by 120 and 400 grades, or 120, 320 and 600 grades can be used. Frequent inspections will determine the progress. Wash and dry the stone, and examine carefully before deciding to go on to the next grit stage. Between grit changes, the cast iron lap should be wiped over with a wet sponge while in motion to clean off all the grit. Before polishing can begin, all traces of silicon carbide grits must be washed

45

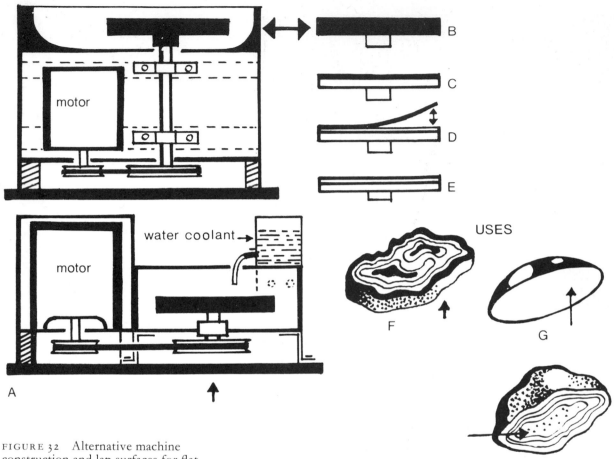

FIGURE 32 Alternative machine
construction and lap surfaces for flat
sections
A Laps can be used with loose grits,
  wet/dry discs, or copper discs used with
  graded diamond particles
B Cast iron lap for use with loose grits
C Copper-faced lap impregnated with
  diamond
D Lap for use with wet/dry discs
E Polishing pad of felt or leather
F Polishing flat slabs
G Base of cabochons
H Sliced nodules polished for display

away from the machine, hands and stone.

Final polishing can be done on a felt or leather disc, or in
some cases an acrylic sheet scored with a knife to retain the
polish is used. Cerium oxide or tin oxide, mixed with water to
a thin paste, are the most widely used polishing agents. Apply
polish as required but do not saturate the disc. Polishing occurs
when the disc is almost dry, but avoid over-heating the stone
by excessive friction (figure 34).

FIGURE 33 Flat section being ground on a cast iron flat lap. Abrasive grit and water applied with a small brush as required

FIGURE 34 Polishing the flat section. The cast iron lap has been replaced by a felt disc on a metal support. The polishing agent can be applied with a brush or squeezy bottle

KEY DIAGRAM TO COLOUR PLATE I
1 Stalactitic agate section
2 Lace agate
3 Jasper
4 Banded agate
5 Smoky quartz, step cut stone
   and rough crystal
6 Brazilian agate
7 Crazy lace agate, with
   drusy quartz crystals
8 Queensland agate
9 Banded agate
10 Citrine, oval brilliant cut stone
   and rough crystal
11 Petrified wood
12 Sodalite
13 Iona marble
14 Tourmaline in quartz
15 Agate
16 Tourmaline, step cut stone
   and rough crystal
17 Amethyst crystals
18 Milky quartz crystals
19 Moss agate, with crystal geode
20 Rhodochrosite
21 Golden tiger's eye
22 Rock crystal, round brilliant cut stone
   and rough crystal
23 Sphalerite (zinc blende) crystals
24 Iron pyrites
25 Rutilated quartz
26 Budstone
27 Amethystine quartz
28 Amethyst, pendeloque cut stone
   and rough crystal

PLATE I Polished stones and natural
crystals

48

Another method of polishing flat slabs is by the use of a vibrating flat lap. This consists of an open circular pan subjected to high speed vibration through the supporting oscillating platform. The rock slabs are placed in the bottom of the pan, which contains abrasive grits, and are ground by the rapid rotary vibration. Thin sections may need to be weighted to give additional downward pressure to assist the abrasive action and speed up the process. Several slabs can be completed at the same time by this method. When the successive abrasive stages are completed, the pan should be thoroughly cleaned. A thick felt pad is then inserted in the pan and impregnated with a suitable polishing agent (figures 35 and 36).

DRILLING STONES

A brief word on drilling holes may be appropriate here, as this can ease many of the setting problems associated with flat sections and other forms of cut. Holes can either be drilled completely through the stones or partially drilled, for purposes

FIGURE 35 (left)   Example of an automatic vibrating lap for processing flat slabs. Fan-cooled motor incorporated. Photograph shows rubber bumper guard to protect edges of slabs. *Star Diamond VL-10. Manufactured by Star Diamond Industries Inc. USA*

FIGURE 36 (right)   Further example of a self-contained vibrating flat lap. Two separate aluminium pans are used; one for abrasives and one for the polishing phase. *Lorton Model FL-15*

49

of attaching rings, pegs or claws.

Abrasive tipped drill bits capable of drilling holes in softer stones are available in many forms and sizes and these can be used in a special chuck on a flexible drive attached to a power drill. For harder stones, including agates and many of the popular stones used by the amateur lapidary, tipped drills of sintered metal and diamond particles are obtainable. These diamond bits can be used effectively in small battery powered hand drills.

Water coolant must be employed during drilling and one suitable method involves the use of a small shallow tray into which a piece of Plasticine is pressed firmly into position. The stone to be drilled is then securely embedded in the Plasticine and just covered with water added to the tray. The drill must be held absolutely steady and free from wobble during the operation, and lifted every few seconds to allow cooling and clearance of stone particles from the hole.

SETTING FLAT SECTIONS

Polished flat sections present many opportunities for creative design and enterprising methods of mounting in jewelry. Among the range of alternatives for brooch and pendant settings, thin slabs trimmed to size and shaped with a geometric outline might suggest a formal design approach (figure 37). In complete contrast, sliced nodules retaining their basic sectional shape and combining natural rough edges with polished faces would call for more imaginative treatment. Sections exposing crystal geodes, used as sparkling decorative features in the stones, have further interesting possibilities.

Methods of securing stones in a piece of jewelry will depend on the perimeter shape, thickness of the slab and natural irregularities which may be conveniently held by pegs or claws. The use of metal strips supporting both sides of the slab, wire prongs, claws and bezels can all be employed to hold the stone in position, and should be related to the general design as a whole. The mounting may be presented as a complete unit or form an integral feature of a more elaborate setting with an extension of related bands of metal and contrasting textured background. These factors can be determined by the basic shape and pattern interest of the stone (figure 38). Where crystals form the dominant pattern element in the slab, these may be sufficiently decorative to require only a thin unobtrusive band of metal wrapped over the edge of the stone to form a setting, or held by wire prongs soldered to a simple base. The problems of suspending a stone as a pendant may be simplified by a groove cut round the side or a hole drilled through the slab.

FIGURE 37 Flat stones cut with pre-determined outlines
A Stones cut with symmetrical axes
   1 Could be set on a metal base of the same shape, and secured by pegs or strips. 2 Bevelled edges assist in setting, and prevent fracturing. 3 Suitable for simple mitred corner box-frame setting, or claws, for rings and cuff-links

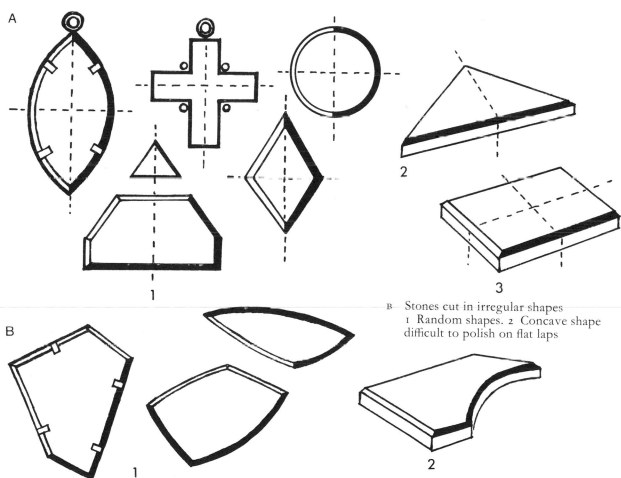

B Stones cut in irregular shapes
   1 Random shapes. 2 Concave shape difficult to polish on flat laps

51

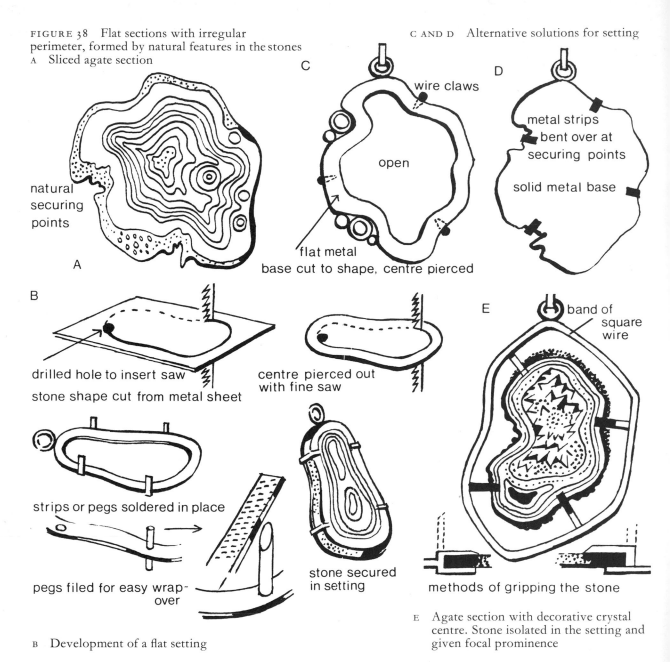

FIGURE 38   Flat sections with irregular
perimeter, formed by natural features in the stones
A   Sliced agate section

C AND D   Alternative solutions for setting

natural
securing
points

A

wire claws

open

flat metal
base cut to shape, centre pierced

metal strips
bent over at
securing points

solid metal base

B

drilled hole to insert saw
stone shape cut from metal sheet

centre pierced out
with fine saw

E   band of
square
wire

strips or pegs soldered in place

pegs filed for easy wrap-
over

stone secured
in setting

methods of gripping the stone

B   Development of a flat setting

E   Agate section with decorative crystal
centre. Stone isolated in the setting and
given focal prominence

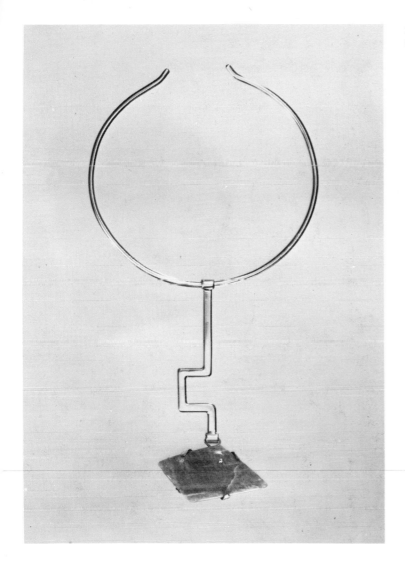

FIGURE 39 Neck ornament in silver with amazonite. *Designed and made by Peter Scarfe*

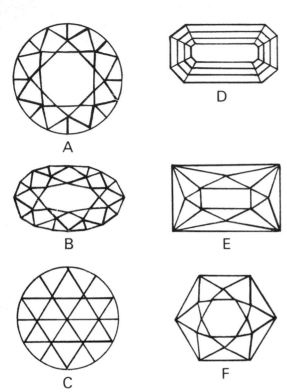

FACETED STONES AND THEIR SETTINGS

Faceted stones display symmetrical patterns of highly polished planes conforming to particular styles of cut (figure 40) and the geometrical arrangement of facet angles is calculated to exploit the refractive properties of the gem mineral. Stones carelessly faceted or cut in a manner not suited to the optical properties of the mineral may result in a loss of light through the lower facets, or scattering of light rays within the stone, dissipating the reflected light values. Reflection, lustre and colour can also be minimised if a stone is imperfectly polished, by diffusion of light on the facet surfaces and such stones will lack sparkle or 'fire'.

Deviation from the standard proportions of a traditional style of facet cut can sometimes be justified when cutting crystals with dark colouration or those which are only lightly tinted. Deeply coloured stones, such as deep red garnet, dark sapphire, and dark green tourmaline, should have a shallow pavilion to give greater illumination within the stone. The appearance of weakly coloured stones can be slightly improved by allowing greater depth to the pavilion. Crystals with patchy colouration or areas of colour zoning should be studied carefully to ensure that such irregularities are placed in the pavilion whenever possible, and not in the crown which should remain clear and evenly tinted. Uneven colour occurring close to the girdle of a stone can sometimes be masked by a cleverly designed setting. Where cutting will permit, a tinted area positioned low in the centre of the pavilion can provide a glow of colour spreading into the crown.

FACETTING EQUIPMENT

By using modern facetting equipment and closely following the correct cutting procedure for a selected style the amateur can soon acquire competence and produce stones equal to those of the professional cutter. Facetting machines are precision-made to enable the operator to work with absolute accuracy when placing a series of facets (figures 41 and 42). The unit

FIGURE 40   Some faceted styles
A   Round brilliant
B   Oval brilliant
C   Rose cut
D   Step cut
E   Cross cut
F   Hexagonal star cut

54

FIGURE 41   Complete facetting unit for precision cutting. Selection of metal dops, 45 degrees angle adaptor and transfer block shown in foreground. *Viking Accura-flex by Geode Industries Inc., New London, Iowa, USA*

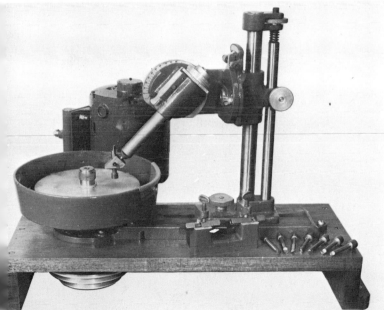

FIGURE 42   Further example of a complete facetting unit. The 45 degrees angle adaptor and dop are positioned in the facetting arm. Two-way transfer block and a selection of metal dops also shown. *Manufactured by A. and D. Hughes Ltd. Warley, Worcestershire*

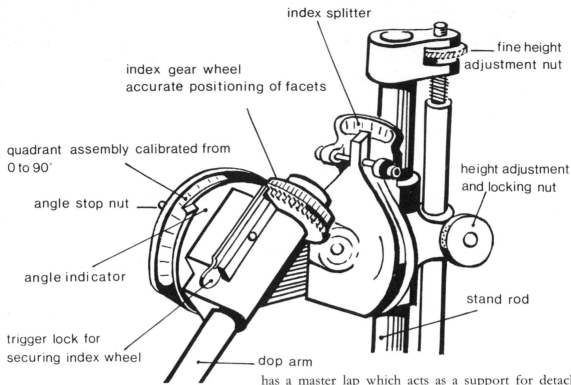

index splitter

fine height
adjustment nut

index gear wheel
accurate positioning of facets

quadrant assembly calibrated from
0 to 90°

angle stop nut

height adjustment
and locking nut

angle indicator

trigger lock for
securing index wheel

stand rod

dop arm

has a master lap which acts as a support for detachable laps and is not a working surface in itself. This is perfectly balanced and turns smoothly on a vertical shaft motivated by belt and pulleys from a $\frac{1}{6}$ hp or $\frac{1}{4}$ hp electric motor. The pulley systems on the motor and master lap assembly should allow varying speeds for cutting and polishing, depending on individual preference and type of material being cut. As a general guide, softer minerals and those of easy cleavage should be cut and polished at slower speeds. The master lap and shaft are mounted on a substantial base which also supports the stand-rod for the facetting head, giving complete rigidity and vertical alignment of shaft and stand. A slot cut in the base enables the stand-rod to be moved backwards and forwards to position the facetting arm correctly in relation to the master lap.

The facetting head assembly (figure 43) which can be elevated or lowered on the stand-rod, consists of a quadrant arc engraved with 90 degrees and a rotating dop arm fitted with a

FIGURE 43 Details of the facetting head assembly from the machine illustrated in figure 42

56

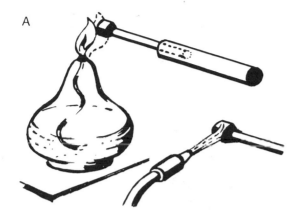

A

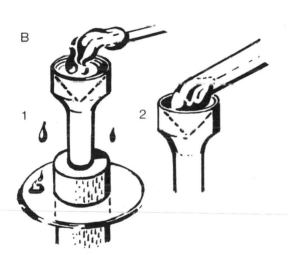

B

C

FIGURE 48 (below) Dopping the pre-form

A Warm the end of a metal dop in the flame of a spirit lamp or propane torch. A holder for the dop is made by drilling a piece of one inch dowel. This protects the fingers from heat

B 1 Hold the metal dop upright and place melted wax in the open end. The dopping wax is heated in a small tin on a hot-plate. As a further protective aid, the illustration shows a small plastic disc which can be slipped over the wooden holder to prevent any droplets of hot wax falling on the hand. 2 Wax can be obtained in stick form. This is heated directly in a flame and inserted in the dop when soft

C 1 The pre-form, previously warmed on the hot-plate, is now pressed into the end of the metal dop until most of the wax has been displaced and the stone is in firm contact with the metal. Level the pre-form, moulding surplus wax under the girdle to give firm support. The wax should not project beyond the girdle. 2 A badly seated stone, supported high on the wax. If any heating occurs during cutting, the stone will move on the softened wax

Shaping the girdle

Before the actual facetting begins it is essential that the girdle of the pre-form is perfectly round. To do this, secure the dop-stick in the chuck of the facetting arm and lower the unit on the stand-rod, placing the arm in a horizontal position with the stone at 90 degrees to the lap. Release the index locking device to allow the facetting arm to rotate freely, switch on the motor and start the drip-feed coolant, or apply grit and water mixture according to type of lap being used. Making careful contact between stone and lap, commence cutting the circular girdle. By slowly turning the dop arm, applying even pressure, and traversing from centre to rim to avoid grooving the lap, continue until the girdle is evenly cut and every part of the circumference will make contact with the lap.

The table

When commencing with the crown, the flat area on top of the stone known as the table is the first part to be cut. A special 45 degree adaptor is used in the chuck to position the top of the dopped stone parallel to the lap surface (figure 49). Lock the index gear to maintain the arm in a fixed position. The motor should be switched on before lowering the facetting head

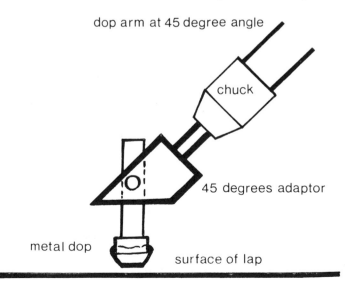

dop arm at 45 degree angle

chuck

45 degrees adaptor

metal dop

surface of lap

FIGURE 49   The 45 degrees angle adaptor

until the stone is in contact with the lap, then commence cutting. It may be found necessary to make fractional alterations by manipulating the height adjustment screw. The table should be cut to about 65 to 70 per cent of the total width of the pre-form at this stage, and will later be reduced to 45 to 50 per cent in the completed stone. Move the stone across the lap during cutting, using plenty of lubricant or frequent applications of grit and water, until the table is perfectly flat. Raise facetting assembly and switch off the motor.

If using a two-stage cutting procedure, remove the first diamond lap and replace with a finer grade. Repeat the cutting action as before to bring the table to a pre-polishing state. For many stones the 800 or 1200 diamond lap may be sufficient to bring the stone to a pre-polish state, omitting the coarser stage. Some facetters, when using loose abrasives on a cast iron lap, use only one grade of grit throughout the cutting stage and continue until the facets are perfectly smooth. This prolongs the cutting time but eliminates the need to clean the machine thoroughly between stages, which is imperative if more than one grit is used. Satisfactory results are obtained by this single grit method, which can be used for all quartz varieties. For harder stones more than one abrasive stage may be necessary prior to polishing.

When the table is quite smooth and scratch-free it can be carefully cleaned ready for polishing. Remove the cutting lap, clearing away all traces of grit if using loose abrasives, and replace with a polishing lap of suitable material. Apply to the revolving lap one of the oxide polishing agents mixed to a thin paste, or diamond compound if preferred. Lower the facetting arm, bringing the 45 degree adaptor with the stone into contact with the lap. Move the stone from side to side as before, applying moderate pressure. Carry out frequent inspections by pivoting the facetting arm upwards, and allow the stone to cool off periodically to prevent frictional heat melting the dopping wax. Frictional heat can be controlled to a certain degree by varying the pressure and polishing speeds. Different positions on the lap, from the centre to outer edge, will provide alternative surface speeds. The fastest speeds occur at the periphery and increase in proportion to the diameter of the

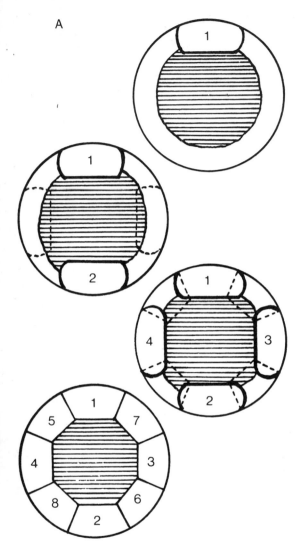

disc. The most suitable speed and polishing position for the stone should be determined by experience. Proceed until a satisfactory polish is achieved. Raise the arm and remove the 45 degree angle adaptor. The dopstick is now fitted directly into the chuck for cutting the main facets.

Crown main facets

The eight main facets can be cut at 42 to 45 degrees for quartz and should be accurately indexed to ensure perfect symmetry. The angle at which the crown main facets are cut will determine the width of the table, and as a rule darkly tinted stones benefit from a wider table by permitting entry of more light. Colourless stones will not suffer from a table of smaller dimensions as considerable light enters from the side facets. Decreasing the angle of the facets will produce a smaller table. Cut opposite pairs of facets for short periods, alternating between the two and frequently comparing their proportions (figure 50). Complete the eight facets, which should form sharp ridges extending from table to girdle. Repeat on a finer grade lap if necessary, or continue until all scratches have been eliminated. Do not polish at this stage.

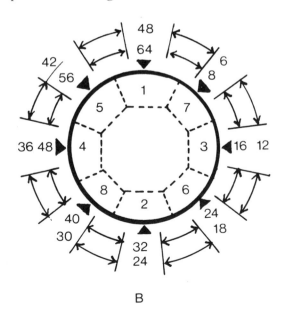

FIGURE 50 Crown main facets
A Progressive sequences in cutting the eight crown main facets, to produce an octagonal table
B Index numbers used for crown mains, using either a 64 tooth, or 48 tooth index gear

Table star facets

The next series of facets to be cut are the eight star facets surrounding the table. These are inverted triangles with the apex reaching one third down the ridges of the mains. The opposite side of the triangle forms the edge of the table, further reducing it to about half the total width of the stone. The star facets are indexed halfway between the position of the main facets and cut at 15 degrees less than the mains. The exact angle, which should be achieved gradually, is the one needed to make the facets touch at the table and have all the points centred and in line with the ridge of the mains. This angle should be carefully recorded so that it can be repeated for any grit changes and the polishing stage. To cut the first star facet, lower the dop arm and stone to the lap for only a second, then lift up and wipe the stone clean with a tissue. Examine the cut carefully with a magnifying lens to determine the progress. The star facets are extremely small and only brief touches to the lap will be sufficient. Gradually progressing round the table, cut and refine the eight facets, but do not polish yet. Proceed to the next series of facets.

FIGURE 51 Development of star and girdle facets to complete the crown of a round standard brilliant
A Eight crown main facets completed
B Eight star facets in position
C Completed crown with sixteen girdle facets added
D Dotted triangle – position of cut for star facet
E Dotted lines – position of girdle facets, relative to completed star facets, shown in black
F Girdle facets, shaded areas

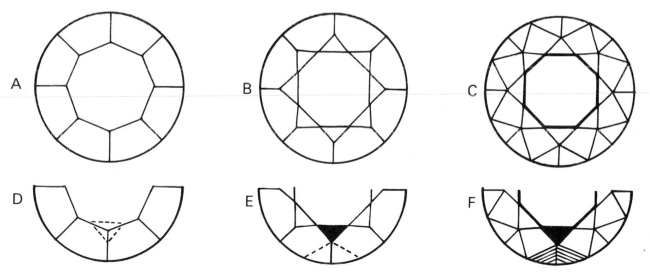

Crown girdle facets

These are sixteen in number, with one on each side of the ridge dividing the main facets, and are indexed in rotation round the girdle. The base of each triangular facet forms the girdle and the apex reaches two-thirds of the distance between girdle and table. The facet angle is a few degrees higher than that used for the main facets. The correct angle should be reached in easy stages to arrive at the required base length to touch round the girdle and to give the necessary apex height. Record the angle reached, for repetition and later polishing stage.

Polishing the crown facets

Pivot the facetting arm upwards, retaining the angle used for the girdle facets. Remove abrasive lap and clean up stone and master lap. Extra care in cleaning is necessary when loose grits have been employed. Attach the polishing lap, start the motor and polish girdle facets in rotation. Apply polishing mixture as required. Inspect the stone frequently to check progress and allow brief cooling periods. It is important to remember that overheating may dislodge the stone from the wax, presenting many problems.

Reset the correct angle for the star facets and continue polishing until completed to satisfaction. Follow with the main facets, with the dop arm set at the required angle, to complete polishing of the full series of crown facets. The stone is now ready for the transfer and re-dopping process in order to cut the pavilion facets.

Use of transfer block

The transfer block, sometimes called transfer jig (figure 52 overleaf) is used as a two-way dopping system to change the stone from one dopstick to another, enabling accurate reversal from crown to pavilion to continue cutting. If the stone should move during cutting, or fall from the dopstick, the transfer block is indispensible for correct re-dopping. The jig consists of two blocks with grooves cut in perfect horizontal alignment, into which two dopsticks are secured with waxed ends facing, one of which holds the stone to be transferred.

Method of transfer

Shown in figures 53 and 54 (overleaf).

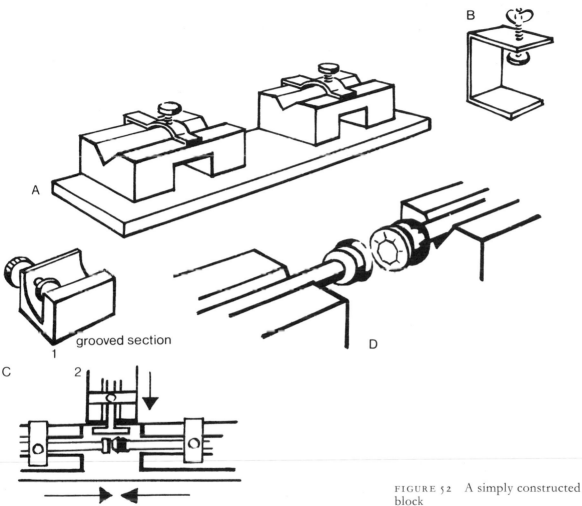

grooved section

FIGURE 52 A simply constructed transfer block

A Two blocks with facing grooves and clamps to secure dops

B Further type of clamp

C 1 Alternative and clamp. 2 Two dops in horizontal alignment. A third block can be used, with a flat face plate, as an accuracy guide

D Dop sticks in the V-shaped grooved blocks

67

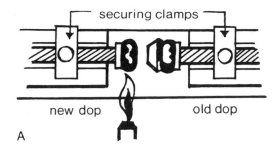

securing clamps

new dop   old dop

A

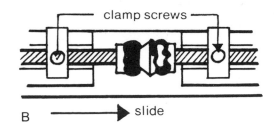

clamp screws

B   → slide

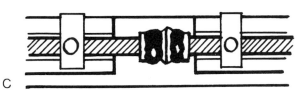

C

FIGURE 53   Transferring a stone, using a transfer block

A   Place dopsticks in V grooves and clamp down. Heat the metal in a low flame, softening the wax on the new dop

B   Release the new dop clamp screw and slide the dop until the soft wax is forced against the crown of the brilliant in the old dop

C   Move the flame along to the wax and metal of the new dop. The metal will retain the heat and keep the wax soft. Release the clamp on the old dop and slide forward until the crown is pressed firmly in position in the new dop wax. Allow to cool and set thoroughly

D   Shows wax leaving the girdle well exposed. Also, the third block in use with flat face plate dop for accurate alignment

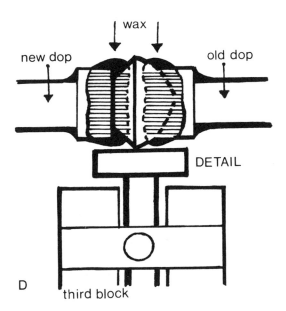

wax

new dop   old dop

DETAIL

D   third block

68

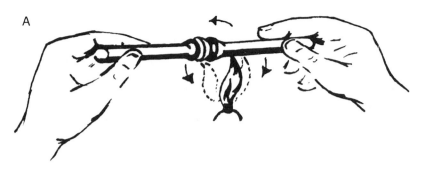

A

old dop

B

new dop

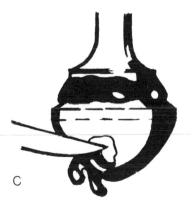

C

FIGURE 54   Transferring a stone,
continued
A   Release the clamps and remove the two
    dops from the block, with the stone
    firmly bonded to both dops by the
    hardened wax. Rotate the old dop in a
    flame, heating the metal and wax until
    the wax becomes soft
B   Ease the old dop away from the pavilion
    end of the pre-form without disturbing
    the new setting
C   The transfer now completed, clean off
    any wax adhering to the stone by
    scraping with a warm knife, or wipe the
    stone with wax solvent, eg methylated
    spirit

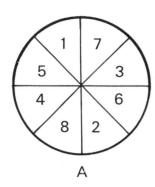

A

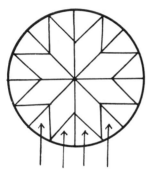

girdle facets

B

Pavilion main facets

The pavilion main facets, which are eight in number, must be accurately lined up with the crown mains. Cut the facets at an angle of about 43 degrees, progressing gradually by cutting opposite facets alternately and checking the symmetry of successive cuts. In the first stages avoid over-cutting the pointed termination of the pavilion and the girdle thickness, which should be about 2 per cent of the width of the stone. Refinements to these can be made at a later stage or on a second lap. Carefully check and record the angles required to complete the series of facets.

Girdle facets

The sixteen pavilion girdle facets are cut at an angle a few degrees higher than the mains. Once again the correct angle should be arrived at gradually until the points of adjacent facets meet at the girdle in the centre of the main facets and extend about halfway from the girdle to the point. Record the correct angle.

Polishing the pavilion facets

All the pavilion facets can now be polished in the usual way, starting with the girdle facets and followed by the pavilion mains. To complete the brilliant, polish the girdle as follows. Lower the facetting arm to a horizontal position with the angle indicator at 90 degrees. Allow the arm to turn freely against the rotating lap, and by gradually turning the stone the whole of the girdle will be polished.

Removing stone from dopstick

Raise the facetting head and remove dop from the chuck. Gently warm the dopstick and soften the wax until the stone can be released from the dop. Remove any wax adhering to the stone, using a heated knife blade or by immersing the stone in a suitable solvent such as methylated spirit.

When sufficient skill and experience has been acquired in cutting standard brilliants of various sizes, it should be possible to attempt the many other styles of facet cuts using a wider selection of gem material.

Care of facetting equipment

Always clean the machine thoroughly after use and wipe over

FIGURE 55   Pavilion facets on a round standard brilliant
A   Pavilion main facets with numbered order of cutting
B   Completed pavilion, with girdle facets added. The girdle facets are situated one at each side of the mains ridge line

with an oily rag any parts susceptible to rusting. Cover the machine to protect from dust. The laps and polishing discs should be carefully stored in separate polythene bags.

MOUNTING FACETED STONES

Settings designed to hold faceted stones must allow maximum light to enter the stones from as many directions as practical from a constructional point of view. Within these limits, the more valuable gemstones must also be given protection from knocks and abrasion and be securely mounted in the piece of jewelry.

FIGURE 56 Double box frame settings
A Construction for rectangular-shaped step cut, with deep pavilion
B End filed to curve of the finger and ring shank
C Basic setting for an oval-shaped brilliant

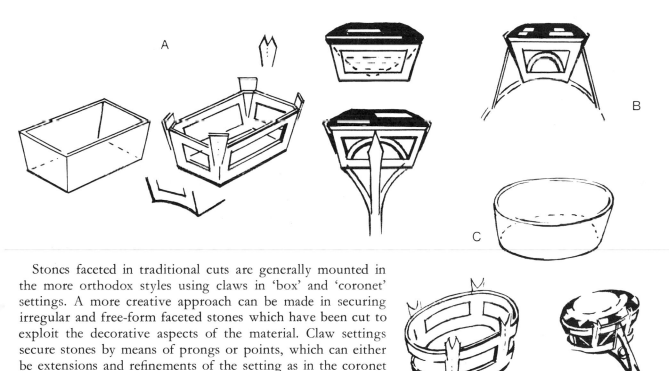

Stones faceted in traditional cuts are generally mounted in the more orthodox styles using claws in 'box' and 'coronet' settings. A more creative approach can be made in securing irregular and free-form faceted stones which have been cut to exploit the decorative aspects of the material. Claw settings secure stones by means of prongs or points, which can either be extensions and refinements of the setting as in the coronet or soldered to supporting shoulders. In the case of the box setting the claws may form part of the structure linking the box frames.

Box settings

This type of setting is suitable for most regular faceted stones which are cut to square or rectangular proportions. A circular or oval shaped box frame setting is used for rounded varieties of cut. Choice of single or double box frames depends on the depth of the stone, with the dimensions of the supporting frames or bearers corresponding to the girdle measurements. In the case of the double frame, the upper band supports the girdle of the stone and the lower band, which is usually of smaller dimensions, protects the pavilion and forms the base of the setting which is attached to the ring shank (figures 57 and 58).

Coronet settings

These are usually associated with brilliant cut stones and are constructed from basic cone shapes, forming crowns or coronets, pierced at the sides to allow passage of light. The upper portion of the cone is filed into a series of points which wrap over the girdle of the stone, securing it in position. The tapering lower part of the setting protects the pavilion and culet (figure 59).

Pavé or bead settings

This is another traditional method of stone setting which can be presented in different ways, involving a variety of tools and skills. Uniform clusters or rows of small stones can be mounted in this way, dispensing with the need for claws. Stones are fitted into depressions sunk into the metal by using a tapered burr, and secured with beads formed by pushing the metal forward with a graver and completed with a beading tool or serrated wheel. A variation on this method is the Thread Setting, where a thread of metal is raised close to the stones with a graver or plain wheel and carefully burnished over the girdle.

FIGURE 57 (above)   Rectangular box frame setting in gold for smoky quartz, step cut with deep pavilion. *Ring setting made by Peter Scarfe*

FIGURE 58 (below)   Oval box frame setting in gold for citrine, oval brilliant cut. *Ring setting made by Peter Scarfe*

overleaf
PLATE 2   Jewelry with polished stones and natural crystals

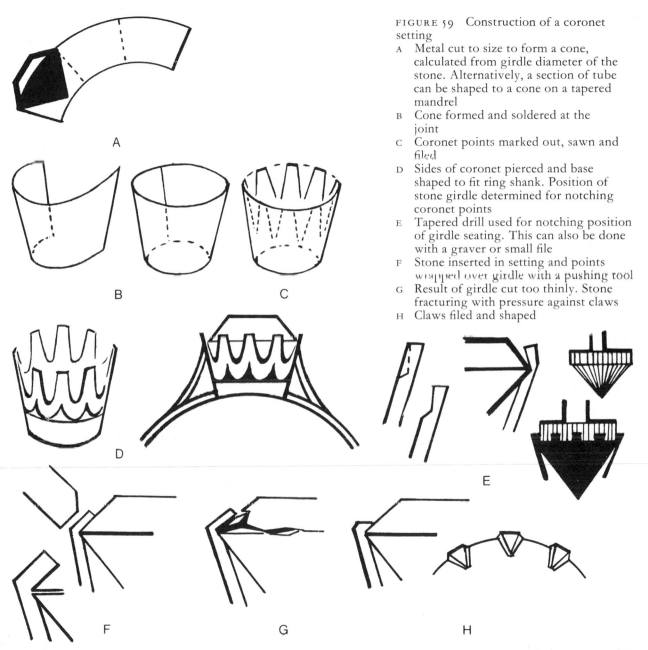

FIGURE 59 Construction of a coronet setting

A   Metal cut to size to form a cone, calculated from girdle diameter of the stone. Alternatively, a section of tube can be shaped to a cone on a tapered mandrel

B   Cone formed and soldered at the joint

C   Coronet points marked out, sawn and filed

D   Sides of coronet pierced and base shaped to fit ring shank. Position of stone girdle determined for notching coronet points

E   Tapered drill used for notching position of girdle seating. This can also be done with a graver or small file

F   Stone inserted in setting and points wrapped over girdle with a pushing tool

G   Result of girdle cut too thinly. Stone fracturing with pressure against claws

H   Claws filed and shaped

73

TUMBLED STONES AND BAROQUE JEWELRY

Tumble-polished stones owe their attraction to the infinite variation of shapes and high degree of polish over the entire surface, including concave areas. Polishing inner curved surfaces by any other method is difficult. A further reason for the popularity of tumbling is the basic simplicity of the process, which simulates the smoothing and rolling action of pebbles on a beach, grinding against each other in the ebb and flow of the tides. The time taken to reduce rocks to pebbles through natural agencies is lengthy, while the mechanical process of tumbling stones in revolving or vibrating containers completes the transformation in a comparatively short period.

The capacity of tumbling barrels can range from pint-size to gallon containers, and some machines are designed to rotate two or three barrels at the same time. Before purchasing a tumbler the operator must decide on space available and the amount of tumbled stones it is possible to use at a particular time. Amassing great quantities of polished stones can create some embarrassment. Also, the larger barrels lead to greater expenditure on grits and polish. The big capacity tumblers are often used by schools and clubs, as well as for commercial purposes.

Rotary tumblers can have either cylindrical or angular barrels (figures 60, 61 and 62), usually constructed of tough polythene or hard rubber, and these are supported between two rollers turning at a very slow speed. The motion gradually lifts the pebble mass within the barrel until the upper layer of stones reach a point of fall and roll down to re-commence the cycle of movement. The initial lift by the flat faces of angular barrels tends to quicken the movement and require a slightly slower speed of rotation to reduce the risk of a throwing action which can fracture some types of stones.

FIGURE 60   Small rotary tumbler with plastic barrel and replaceable rubber liner. Gasket-sealed, screw-on lid. *Star Diamond MT-3*

FIGURE 61 (below left)   Tumbler with two round plastic barrels which operate simultaneously. Rollers turned by a belt from the large pulley to a motor mounted in the rear. Photograph shows a small belt linking the two rollers. *Kernowcraft Model KR 2*

FIGURE 62 (below right)   Rotary tumbler with angular barrel. A heavy duty rubber liner, which is removable, contains the load within the barrel. The ends are sealed with a gasket and wing nuts. *Highland Park Model KCB-10*

The barrel load is composed of either selected beach pebbles or imported rock offcuts and hammered pieces, which should be of the same hardness (Mohs' scale). Different sizes of stones are used to advantage in the same load, as smaller stones will help to grind into hollows in larger stones. The size of stones used should be proportionate to the size of tumbler barrel and, as a rough guide, not exceeding one and a half inches in length or diameter in a one gallon capacity barrel.

A measured quantity of silicon carbide abrasive grit is added at each phase and the whole load covered with water. Three abrasive stages are usual, followed by a polishing phase and a final detergent rinse. The grit size combinations and length of tumbling time depends on such factors as hardness and surface condition of the stones. The following table will provide a working guide for the beginner but are not intended as hard and fast rules. As experience is gained it will be appreciated that successful tumbling results are mainly related to careful supervision during the operation and quality of stones being processed. The quantities of silicon carbide grit suggested are for a 1 gallon (4.5 litres) barrel with a load of 6 lb to 8 lb (3 kg to 4 kg) of stones.

Phase 1 80 or 120 grit $\frac{3}{4}$ lb to 1 lb (340 g to 454 g)
Phase 2 220 or 320 grit $\frac{1}{2}$ lb to $\frac{3}{4}$ lb (227 g to 340 g)
Phase 3 400 or 500 grit $\frac{1}{2}$ lb to $\frac{3}{4}$ lb (227 g to 340 g)
Phase 4 Polishing agent 6 oz to 8 oz (170 g to 227 g)
Phase 5 Final rinse $\frac{1}{2}$ to 1 cup of detergent powder and water.

For water-worn pebbles and pre-forms, allow four to seven days for each abrasive stage. Rough material and hammered rock may take two to three weeks at the first stage with 80 grit, which may need to be renewed, and four to seven days at subsequent stages. Polishing usually takes up to four days, and a detergent rinse for four hours will complete the operation.

Tumbler barrels should be loaded to half or two-thirds capacity, bearing in mind the important factors of stone size and density. If the load is too light the stones will not tumble effectively and the sliding action will produce flattened stones. It is advisable to record the weight of a batch of stones before

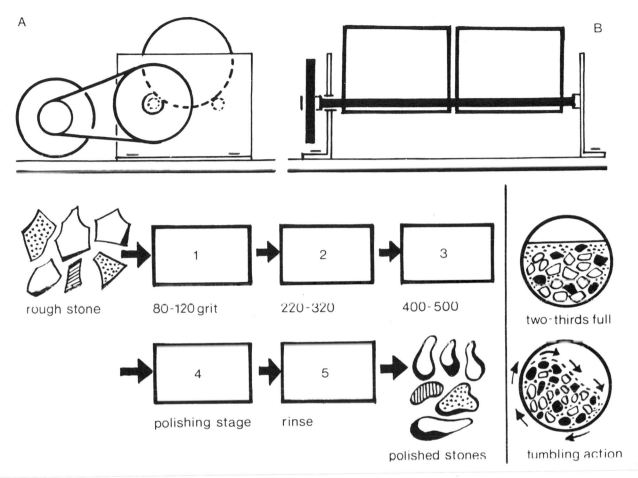

rough stone   80-120 grit   220-320   400-500

polishing stage   rinse   polished stones

two-thirds full

tumbling action

adding the grit, and to carry out weight checks between grit changes. During tumbling, the abrasive action of the grits, particularly the coarser grades, will considerably reduce the load and the original weight should be made up by adding smooth flints or tumbled stones which have reached a similar stage. Tumbling should be a continuous operation but frequent checks must be carried out to ascertain the state of the load and, if necessary, a little more water may be added to lessen viscosity. It is only necessary to wash and inspect a handful of stones to evaluate the progress made. Much has been written about the

FIGURE 63 Progressive tumbling phases with a rotary tumbler
A   End view of tumbler, showing V belt drive
B   Twin barrels on rollers

build-up of gasses inside tumbler barrels, but this rarely occurs if regular twentyfour-hourly checks are carried out. Some operators include a small quantity of baking-powder in the load to counteract the formation of gas. The possibility of gas forming is usually associated with unlined metal drums, and the use of polythene, polyvinyl and rubber tumbler barrels presents fewer problems of this kind.

Between phases, stones and barrels must be washed thoroughly and the accumulated sludge disposed of in polythene bags or placed in a hole dug in the garden. Tumbling waste must never be allowed to go into the household drainage system because of the cement-like properties of the sludge. When grit phases are completed and the stones perfectly smooth, polishing can be carried out. A polishing agent such as cerium oxide or tin oxide is used, together with additives in the form of plastic granules, cork or leather scraps to cushion the load. A final rinse with clear water and a little detergent in the barrel will remove any filmy deposits from the polished stones.

VIBRATORY TUMBLERS

The hoppers or containers, which are usually cast in light metal alloy with thick polyvinyl lining, remain in a fixed position. Instead of tumbling in the accepted sense, the batch of stones is subjected to high-speed vibration, producing rapid agitation of the load, and in addition there is a gradual rotation of the whole mass of stones within the container. Unlike normal tumblers, where half to one third of the space within the barrel must be clear for the tumbling action, the hoppers should be filled to near capacity. The complete grinding and polishing cycle is speeded up during the vibratory process and a batch of stones can be completed in two to five days. During the operation the rate of vibration can be in excess of 2500 per minute and the load, with abrasive charge, remains in a state of suspension, supported in a thickened solution containing minimum moisture. The stones are evenly coated with the abrasive emulsion and, as viscosity reduces the impact of stones against each other, it is possible to process material of different hardness at the same time with little weight loss or danger of fracturing.

FIGURE 64 (opposite above)   Vibratory tumbler with single hopper mounted on the vibrating platform. *Viking Vibra-sonic Model VT-14*

FIGURE 65 (opposite below)   Vibratory tumbler with twin hoppers, detachable for load changes and cleaning. Containers have seal-tight lids for easy inspection of contents during tumbling. *Viking Vibra-sonic Model VT-12*

Prepare a load which is evenly balanced in variable sizes of stones and proportion of rock types, ensuring that up to 25 per cent consists of smaller stones 19 mm to 13 mm ($\frac{3}{4}$ in. to $\frac{1}{2}$ in.), to fill the spaces between those of larger diameter. The load should occupy 75 per cent to 80 per cent of the total capacity of the container. The weight of the stones should be recorded, together with amounts of abrasive and water added. A low moisture content assists the abrasive and polishing actions, and chemical additives in tablet form act as an emulsifying or water thickening agent to give a slippery quality to the batter-like mixture. Other thickening materials can be used such as ground-rice powder or dehydrated potato powder, and a suitable consistency achieved through trial and error. Additional thickening agent should be used when polishing softer or easily fractured stones. Inspection of the load should be carried out at eight-hourly intervals, and if the mixture has over-thickened to a viscous sludge from accumulated grinding waste a little more water can be added.

Two or three grit phases can be used and, as in normal tumbling operations, the stones and containers must be washed thoroughly between grit changes. Ideally, a separate hopper should be kept exclusively for the final polishing stage to avoid any risk of grit contamination. During the pre-polish and final polish the usual additives such as plastic granules, vermiculite or crushed nut shells are used as filling material to cushion the stones. The quantities of grit, polish and water used at each stage are not suggested here as manufacturers of vibratory tumblers supply details of amounts recommended specifically for their machines. It is advisable to record such vital factors as load weights, stone varieties, quantities of grit and moisture used for future reference and comparison of results.

MOUNTING TUMBLE-POLISHED STONES

The extensive range of manufactured fittings and jewellers' findings now available has added to the simplicity of mounting tumbled stones in jewelry. Finished pieces can be assembled without previous knowledge or skill, and the basic tools involved are limited to a small pair of smooth-jawed pliers, tweezers and a strong, colourless adhesive. Other items of equipment can be devised as aids, such as a Plasticine base for holding stones (figure 66 overleaf) or an inverted nail-brush for supporting rings in the bristles during setting of adhesive. A simple wooden frame can be used to suspend a length of bracelet chain to facilitate the fixing of bell caps and jump rings (figure 67 overleaf).

Findings

This is a term applied to many of the miscellaneous small items supplied for jewelry purposes and a few of these, necessary for assembling pendants and bracelets are briefly described.

Bell caps to fit the tapered end of tumbled stones are manufactured in many sizes and styles. Claws, petals and leaves, with pierced or filigree designs, form a range of decorative elements. A loop or ring is incorporated for attachments.

Jump rings are circles of wire with a break in the circumference which can be opened and closed with small pliers for attachment or linking purposes.

Spring bails   A flattened loop of metal with a divided overlap for springing open and shut. A spring bail can be attached to a bell cap and a pendant chain threaded through the loop of the bail to run freely.

Bolt rings   A type of circular fastener used to secure two ends of a chain.

Chains   These can be bought made up in standard lengths or obtained by the yard and are graded by the size and weight of the links. A light trace chain, 406 mm or 457 mm (16 in. or 18 in.) long, can be used for pendants with small stones, worn fairly high. Larger stones may require medium or heavy chain for additional support, in lengths from 508 mm (20 in.) upwards. Chain bought by the yard and divided into lengths would require a linking jump ring to form a continuous chain; or a jump ring at each of the two free ends, one of which is attached to a bolt ring, when making a chain to unfasten.

Assembling a pendant

Requirements   Tumbled stone, bell cap of suitable proportions, jump ring or spring bail, length of chain, adhesive.

Mould the bell cap prongs on the tumbled stone to conform

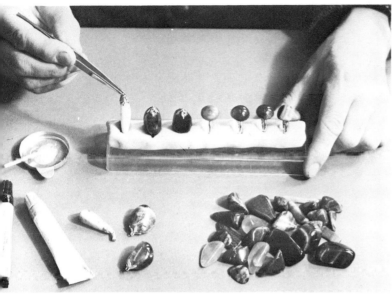

FIGURE 66 Stones and rings supported in plasticine during fixing and setting period. A bell cap is being attached to a tumbled stone with the aid of tweezers. In the foreground: tubes of adhesive, stones with bell caps and a selection of tumbled stones

FIGURE 67 Simple aid to hold chain taut and assist spacing when using jump rings to attach stones with bell caps

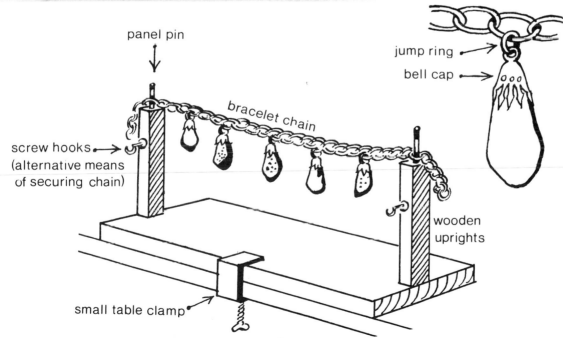

panel pin

bracelet chain

screw hooks
(alternative means
of securing chain)

jump ring

bell cap

wooden
uprights

small table clamp

to the irregular shape, making sure the loop is facing front, and remove. With a small piece of emery paper or similar abrasive, remove the shine from the tip of the stone where the bell cap will be attached. (The adhesive will not stick firmly on a shiny surface.) Support the stone upright as shown in figure 66 and mix a small quantity of adhesive. With a pointed match-stick, apply adhesive to the bell cap sparingly. Holding the bell cap with tweezers, gently press into position on the stone. Allow the adhesive to set thoroughly.

Select a jump ring or spring bail, open with pliers and attach to loop of the bell cap. Close the ring or loop. The stone and bell cap now has a movable ring or loop through which a chain can be threaded. If a continuous chain is desired, the two free ends are linked with a small jump ring. To fix a bolt ring, select two jump rings – one slightly smaller than the other. Open the smaller jump ring and attach to the chain and loop on the bolt ring. Affix the larger jump ring to the other end of the chain to engage the bolt ring fastener.

Making a chain bracelet

Requirements Small tumbled stones, bell caps, jump rings, bolt ring, heavy or patterned chain of suitable length for wrist.

Follow the same procedure as used in making a pendant. Fix bell caps to stones. Bell caps are then attached to chain at regular intervals with jump rings. Add a clasp fastener or bolt ring to secure the ends of the chain. Chain can be kept taut on a wooden frame (figure 67).

Flat pad bracelet

These consist of linked pads which are sold complete with fastener. Selected tumbled stones, flattened on one side or carefully sliced on a trim-saw, are stuck on the pads to complete the bracelet.

Other types of ready-made fittings for jewelry include rings and brooches with flat or frilled pads, many different kinds of earrings, cuff-links, tie-clips and countless items for ornamental purposes involving the use of tumbled stones (figure 68).

The adhesive used should be suitable for cementing stones to metal and manufacturer's instructions carefully followed with regard to mixing and length of time for curing. When set, the adhesive should be colourless and waterproof.

FIGURE 68 (opposite) Selection of manufactured jewelry fittings:
Left Completed pendant
Top Completed bracelet
Second row Bell caps, jump rings, bolt rings, key chain, tie clip
Third row Brooch and rings
Fourth row Cuff links
Fifth row Tie-tack, ear-ring fittings
Bottom three rows Bracelet chain and pads

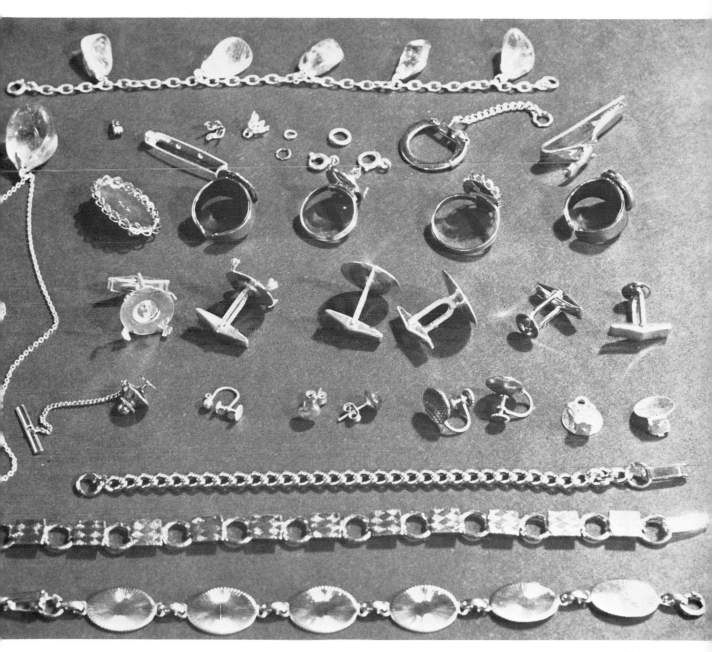

NATURAL CRYSTALS IN JEWELRY

Many types of natural crystals can be used in jewelry without any cutting or shaping, and the crystal faces provide excellent reflective surfaces in much the same way as faceted stones. The crystal shape or habit is determined by the molecular structure of the mineral or combination of minerals; for example, fluorite crystalises in cubes whereas silica, in the crystalline quartz varieties, displays a series of hexagonal prisms with pointed terminations. Crystal variations are endless and within any specific mineral group it is possible to find contrasts of larger forms surrounded by clusters of minute or drusy growths of repetitive shape, as well as isolated single crystals. Twinning, where crystals are closely joined, and inter-penetration of one crystal by another, adds to the surface interest when used as decorative units in jewelry.

Some of the most durable small groups of crystals are of crystalline quartz, including rock crystal, amethyst, citrine and smoky quartz, and these are reasonably easy to obtain. Although often forming crystal groups of a size suitable for jewelry, fluorite and calcite would be too vulnerable because of their softness and easy cleavage. Well-formed iron pyrite crystals, having a yellow, brassy lustre, are very attractive in settings. The glittering black crystals of specular haematite and those of sphalerite or zinc blende, look equally good when set in silver mounts. Small pieces of ruby in zoisite and chalcedony 'roses' covered with tiny quartz crystals are frequently seen in modern jewelry settings (figure 69).

Mounting crystals, whether singly or in clusters, calls for some ingenuity. By examining the specimens and determining the most advantageous securing points, claws, bezels and wires can be used in a manner to suit the particular character of the crystals. With some varieties the matrix holding the crystals can often be sliced and trimmed on a diamond saw, and carefully shaped on a grinding wheel. In this way it is possible to cut a pre-determined perimeter shape for a more formal setting.

FIGURE 69   Pendant with *chalcedony rose* set in silver

84

DESIGN

Although styles in jewelry design have altered throughout the ages, basic methods of securing stones have changed little. Fashion and tradition have also influenced the acceptance and use of specific gem minerals, and the formal precision of established cuts has often imposed limitations on the over-all designs. The reflected brilliance of faceted stones is usually sufficient as a decorative focal element and further enrichment of the settings may be unnecessary.

The choice of stones and other decorative materials now available has broadened the scope of present-day jewellers, and designers will incorporate these in the most imaginative and satisfying way. A creative approach to jewelry design is often suggested by natural qualities of shape, pattern and colour present in ornamental stones. Crystal forms and free-style cuts offer similar opportunities, and the evolution of appropriate settings should display a harmonious and studied relationship. Exploration of colour alone may provide a satisfactory departure with stones selected for subtle contrast, quiet harmony or startling impact, depending on the purpose of the piece of jewelry. Further possibilities of combining enamels or coloured resins should be considered.

For the over-all design of a piece of jewelry, decorative features chosen from natural sources can supply an inexhaustible fund of reference, and the regular use of such aids as sketch-book, camera and microscope will assist close observations and assimilation of pattern elements. Stylization of natural forms can be suitably adapted as a basis for jewelry settings, while geometric and abstract arrangements are evolved by manipulation of shapes into balanced units. Contrasts of scale, stability of straight lines with fluidity of curves, solid and pierced areas, and variation of textured surfaces all provide unlimited interest to offset the stones.

Experimental techniques further influence design possibilities in providing imaginative supports and backgrounds for precious stones. Random arrangements of fused metal scraps

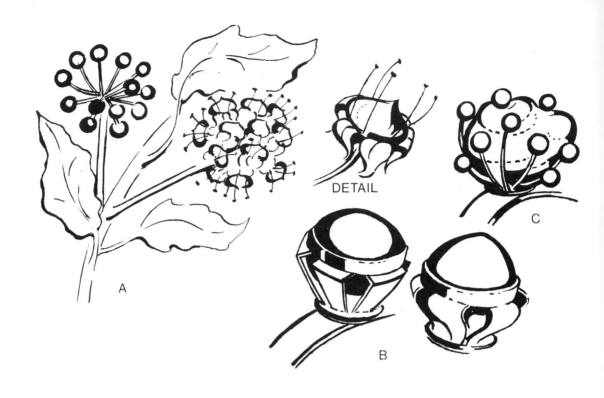

DETAIL

FIGURE 70 Natural forms as a design basis
A Flowers and berries of a variety of ivy, with enlarged flower detail
B Jewelry settings suggested by the flower detail
C Setting for an irregular-shaped stone, based on the cluster formation of berries

and the exploitation of freely cast and etched shapes will introduce an element of spontaneity and discovery. In sharp contrast, machined precision of base and precious metals turned on a lathe will impose additional character when in the hands of a sensitive and disciplined designer.

In brief, a working knowledge of basic materials and methods, linked with keen visual awareness, are necessary attributes of

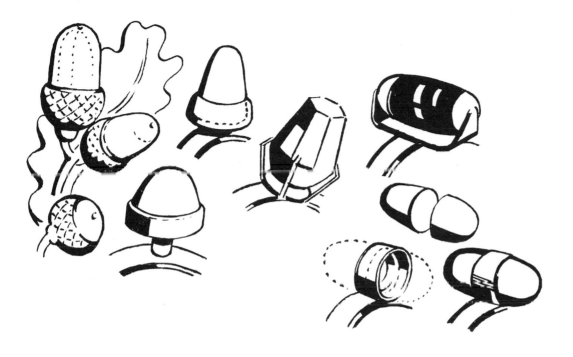

all creative crafts, enabling the designer to develop ideas within the limitations of the selected media. The jeweller is working with responsive metals which can be sawn, hammered, filed and polished, in association with gemstones and other forms of applied decoration. However fashioned, it is important that the basic character of the materials and the specific function of the final product should not be lost or obscured.

FIGURE 71   Modified cup and acorn themes, for shaped stones in ring settings

87

FIGURE 72
A   Analysis of pine cone details, enlarged
    as a pendant design
B   Leaf silhouette pattern given added
    interest by adjusting the symmetry, and
    development as a design which could
    combine enamelling with set stones

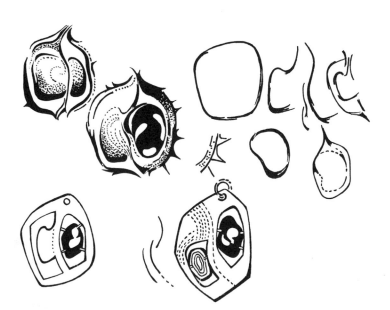

FIGURE 73   Designs suggested by sections
of a horse-chestnut

88

Jewelry is designed to be worn as a costume accessory, providing a striking decorative feature on a ground of contrasting material or simply a subtle link with other matching accessories. Quite often a piece of jewelry is worn as a flamboyant expression of the owners' personality. Finger rings and, to a lesser degree, pendants are rarely static, while brooches have only a limited mobility depending on the activity of the wearer. This factor can directly influence the choice and cut of stones; for example the movement of a faceted stone in a ring presents an ever-changing pattern of light and colour. Softer varieties of stones are more susceptible to knocks and abrasion and may be more suitable for setting in a less active situation or afforded additional protection within the basic construction. Jewelry with limited movement is often subject to closer scrutiny and may require a more decorative type of stone or elaboration of the setting.

The approach to problems of design is often a very personal one and the accompanying diagrams and sketches, which illustrate the design processes and indicate the growth of ideas from natural and abstract sources, may serve as a starting point. The orthodox cutting and setting techniques outlined in previous chapters will help the beginner to establish a basis for further experimentation.

FIGURE 74 Abstract arrangements which can be planned with cut paper or card

A Strip units showing progressive design interest. Variety is achieved by different widths and levels in the overall arrangement. This creates interesting background shapes

B Similar development using curved shapes and an example of contrast which can be created by using curves with straight lines

C Arrangement of larger masses, with interest developing away from formal symmetry. The final solution shows a balanced and varied unit

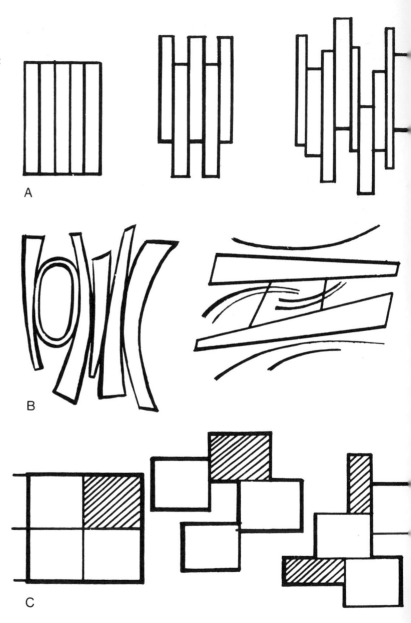

FIGURE 75

A The rigid symmetry of the two squares and enclosed areas provides little visual stimulus

B Interest can be greatly increased by positioning the inner square off-centre

C Further variations in design can be developed by introducing irregular shapes and ovals

D These irregular shapes may correspond to pierced areas with bezels and set stones

JEWELRY TOOLS AND MATERIALS

This is a summary of minimum requirements for jewelry-making. Many other specialised tools can be added to the workshop as experience is gained and new techniques are developed. It is not necessary to set up an elaborate workshop to make small pieces of jewelry; a sturdy kitchen table can be used as a workbench.

METALS AND SOLDERS

Gilding metal, copper and silver, in the form of sheet and wire, are obtainable in a range of thicknesses or standard gauges. Wire is available in round, half-round and square section. Solders are supplied in different grades, having varying melting points: 1 Enamel, 2 Hard, 3 Medium, 4 Easy. When more than one soldering operation is required, solders should be used in order from hard to soft. The easy and medium solders are usually sufficient for simple operations.

Flux, in the form of borax cone or powder, or a liquid preparation, is used to allow free flowing of the solder and prevent oxidation on the heated metal.

HEATING

Traditional mouth blowpipe and gas flame, or various types of torches using butane or propane bottled gas.

SOME BASIC EQUIPMENT

Adjustable piercing saw frame and saw blades   The fine blades allow cutting of intricate shapes and curves. The saw is held in a vertical position and cuts on the downward stroke, with the metal held horizontally.

Hand drill and assorted drill bits   Many functions, including drilling holes in metal to insert piercing saw blade prior to sawing.

Tinman's snips   For cutting solder and small strips of metal.

Pliers, various   Snipe nose, round nose and flat nose. Many uses, including bending metal and twisting wires.

Files   Hand files 102 mm and 152 mm (4 in. and 6 in.) smooth cut and half-round. An assortment of needle files in various section shapes. Rifflers, curved files used for areas difficult to reach with straight files.

Small hammers Ball pein, rawhide mallet. For bending and levelling strips of metal on stakes, round triblets and on metal blocks.

Vices Fixed bench vice. Hand vices for detailed work, such as pin vice and ring stick or ring clamp.

Vee shaped bench peg This is screwed or clamped to the work-bench to facilitate filing and use of piercing saw.

Miscellaneous items Charcoal blocks or asbestos pads, used as supports during soldering, or the work can be placed on a wire soldering wig. A fine camel-hair brush can be used to apply flux to the joints and pick up the small pieces of solder known as *paillons*. Tweezers are useful for placing small pieces of metal in position for soldering. Emery sticks and fine abrasive papers remove scratches and file marks, and can be used to clean the metal ready for soldering. Water of Ayr stone and pumice powder will smooth the surface of the work before polishing. A burnisher of polished steel, or a tapered polished agate set in a metal holder, is used to burnish the wrap-over portion of a bezel when setting cabochons.

ACID BATH OR 'PICKLE'

Following soldering or annealing, which is a heating process to make the metal more malleable, discolouration occurs from oxidation. This is removed by immersing the metal in a solution of diluted acid. A solution of 1 part sulphuric acid to 10 parts water is usually sufficient for most purposes. ALWAYS ADD ACID TO WATER when preparing the solution, NEVER THE OTHER WAY ROUND. Tongs or tweezers used for removing work from the 'pickle' must be made of brass or copper. A container of clean water should be available for rinsing the work when it is taken out of the acid.

POLISHING

The surface of the work is finally polished, either by hand or on electrically-powered polishing buffs, using tripoli, crocus and jewellers' rouge in bar form as polishing agents.

FURTHER READING

Collecting and Polishing Stones   HERBERT SCARFE   B. T.
Batsford, London 1970

Comprehensive Faceting Instructions   D. L. HOFFMAN   Aurora
Lapidary Books, USA 1968

Facet Cutters Handbook   E. J. SOUKUP   Gembooks,
California, USA 1962

Gemcraft   LELANDE QUICK AND HUGH LEIPER   Pitman,
London and Chilton, Philadelphia 1960

Gem Cutting   J. SINKANKAS   Van Nostrand Co., USA 1962

Gems and Gemmology   C. J. PARSONS AND E. J. SOUKUP
Gembooks, California, USA 1961

Gems, their sources, descriptions and identification   R. WEBSTER FGA
Butterworths, London and Shoe String, Hamden,
Connecticut 1962.

Handmade Jewellery   A. R. EMERSON   Dryad Press, Leicester
1953

Jewellery Making for the Amateur   KLARES LEWES   B. T.
Batsford, London 1965

Jewels   P. J. FISHER   B. T. Batsford, London 1965

Making Jewellery, an introduction   K. J. HARTWELL   Hulton
Educational Publications, London 1967

Minerals and Man   CORNELIUS S. HURLBUT JR,
Thames & Hudson, London and Random House, NY 1969

Minerals and Rocks in Colour   J. F. KIRKALDY   Blandford
Press, London 1963

Minerals, Rocks and Gemstones   RUDOLF BORNER
Oliver & Boyd, Edinburgh and Dufour, Chester Springs,
Pennsylvania 1962

AUSTRALIAN PUBLICATIONS

Australian Gem Hunters' Guide   K. J. BUCHESTER   Ure Smith
1965

Australian Lapidary Guide   K. J. BUCHESTER   Ure Smith 1967

Australian Rocks Minerals and Gemstones   R. O. CHALMERS
Angus and Robertson 1967

The Opal Book   FRANK LEECHMAN   Ure Smith 1961

How to find Australian Gemstones   DERRICK AND DOUG STONE
Periwinkle 1969

Minerals Rocks and Gems – A Handbook for Australia
J. A. TALEN   Jacaranda 1970

LAPIDARY MAGAZINES

Gems – The British Lapidary Magazine   BI-MONTHLY
29 Ludgate Hill, London EC4

The Canadian Rockhound   BI-MONTHLY   Vancouver, B.C.
Canada

The Lapidary Journal   MONTHLY   California, USA

Gems and Minerals   MONTHLY   California, USA

Rock and Gem   BI-MONTHLY   California, USA

Australian Lapidary Magazine   BI-MONTHLY

VISUAL AID

Colour Filmstrip on Lapidary Techniques with teaching notes
COMPILED BY HERBERT SCARFE   Published by EP Group
of Companies, East Ardsley, Wakefield, Yorkshire,
England.

SUPPLIERS OF LAPIDARY EQUIPMENT AND MATERIALS

UNITED KINGDOM

Allcraft 11 Market Street, Watford, WD1 7AA

Ammonite Limited Llandow, Cowbridge, Glamorgan, Wales

Art and Crafts Unlimited 49 Shelton Street, London WC2

ML Beach (Products) Limited 41 Church Street, Twickenham, Middlesex

Brydon 18 Wordsworth Road, Colne, Lancashire

Candlemakers Supplies 4 Beaconsfield Terrace Road (off Blythe Road) London W14

Craftorama 14 Endell Street, London WC2

Derwent Crafts 50 Stonegate, York

Gariffe Gem Company Holmridge, Rocky Road, Gilnahirk, Co. Down

Gemrocks Limited 7/8 Holborn, London EC1 (Distributors for Geode Industries Inc. USA)

Gemset of Broadstairs 31 Albion Street, Broadstairs, Kent

Gemstones 44 Walmsley Street, Hull HU3 1QD (Agent for MK Diamond Blades)

Gemstonex 9 Bapton Lane, Exmouth, Devon

Glenjoy Lapidary Supplies 89 Westgate, Wakefield, Yorkshire

Hirsh Jacobson 91 Marylebone High Street, London W1

A. & D. Hughes Limited Popes Lane, Oldbury, Warley, Worcestershire

Kernowcraft Rocks and Gems Limited 44 Lemon Street, Truro, Cornwall

Keystones 1 Local Board Road, Watford, Herts and Antique Supermarket, 3 Barrett Street, London W1

Manninart Colby, Isle of Man

AT Nunn 5 Pool Valley, Brighton 1, Sussex

Kenneth Parkinson, FGA 11 Fitzroy Street, Hull HU5 1LL,

Pebblegems 51 King James Avenue, Cuffley, Potters Bar, Herts

PMR Lapidary Equipment and Supplies Atholl Road, Pitlochry, Perthshire, Scotland

RFD Parkinson & Co. Limited Doulting, Shepton Mallet, Somerset

The Rockhound Shop The White House, 66 Front Street, Newbiggin-by-the-Sea, Northumberland

Scotrocks Partners 48 Park Road, Glasgow C4 and 120–122 Rose Street, South Lane, Edinburgh

Solent Lapidary (R and MA Gould) 145 Highland Road, Southsea, Hampshire

Stones and Settings 54 Main Street, Prestwick, Ayrshire

Sutherland Gemcutters Achmelvich by Lairg, Sutherland, Scotland

Tideswell Dale Rock Shop (Don Edwards) Tideswell, Derbyshire

Wessex Gems and Crafts Longacre, Downs Road, South Wonston, Winchester, Hampshire

Whithear Lapidary Company 35 Ballards Lane, London N3

AUSTRALIA

Lapidary supply firms are listed in the Pink Pages of the telephone directories.

US

Consult the Yellow Pages of the local telephone directories under 'precious and semiprecious stones,' or write to the following for their catalog:

Stones

Geode Industries Inc 106/108 West Main Street, New London, Iowa

T. B. Hagstoz & Son 709 Sansom Street, Philadelphia, Pennsylvania 19106

Highlands Park Manufacturing Division – MK Diamond Products Division, Musto Industries Inc 12600 Chadron Avenue, Hawthorne, California 90250

International Gem 15 Maiden Lane, New York, NY 10038

Nathan Gem & Pearl Company Inc 18 East 48 Street, New York, NY 10017

Star Diamond Industries Inc 1421 West 240 Street, Harbor City, California 90710

Findings

T. B. Hagstoz & Son *as above*

Krieger & Dranoff 44 West 47 Street, New York, NY 10036

American Handicraft Company Inc 20 West 14 Street, New York, NY 10011

Tools

T. B. Hagstoz & Son *as above*

Allcraft 22 West 48 Street, New York, NY 10036

Anchor Tool & Supply Company Inc 12 John Street, New York, NY 10038

The Craftool Company Wood-Ridge, New Jersey 07075